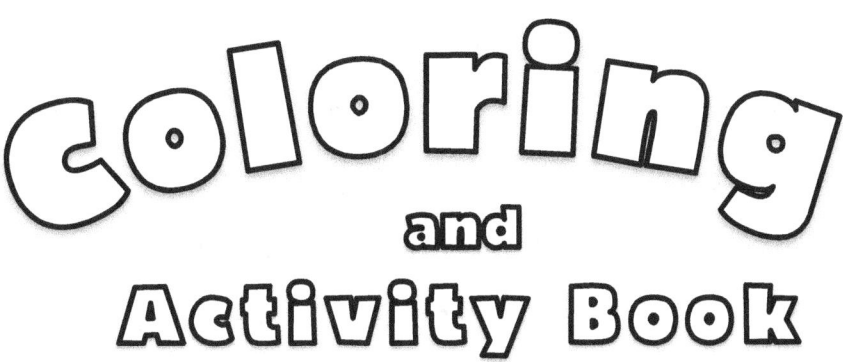

Coloring
and
Activity Book

This book belongs to:

_____

_____

As is the case with most coloring books, you will find that the reverse side of each coloring page is intentionally colored a light gray and left blank to help prevent bleed-through to the following page. We suggest that you place a plain piece of paper or thin cardboard between pages to preserve your artwork.

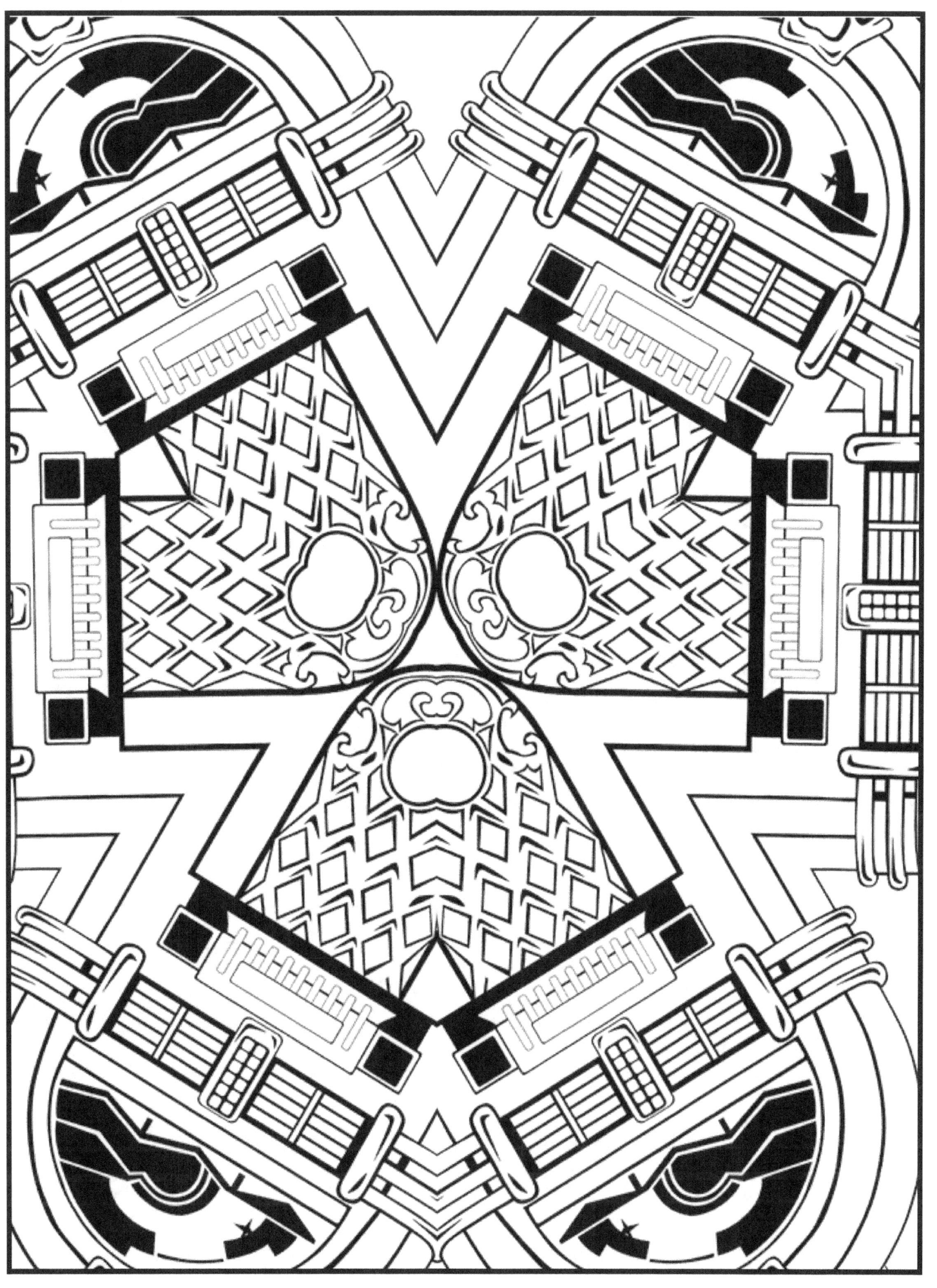

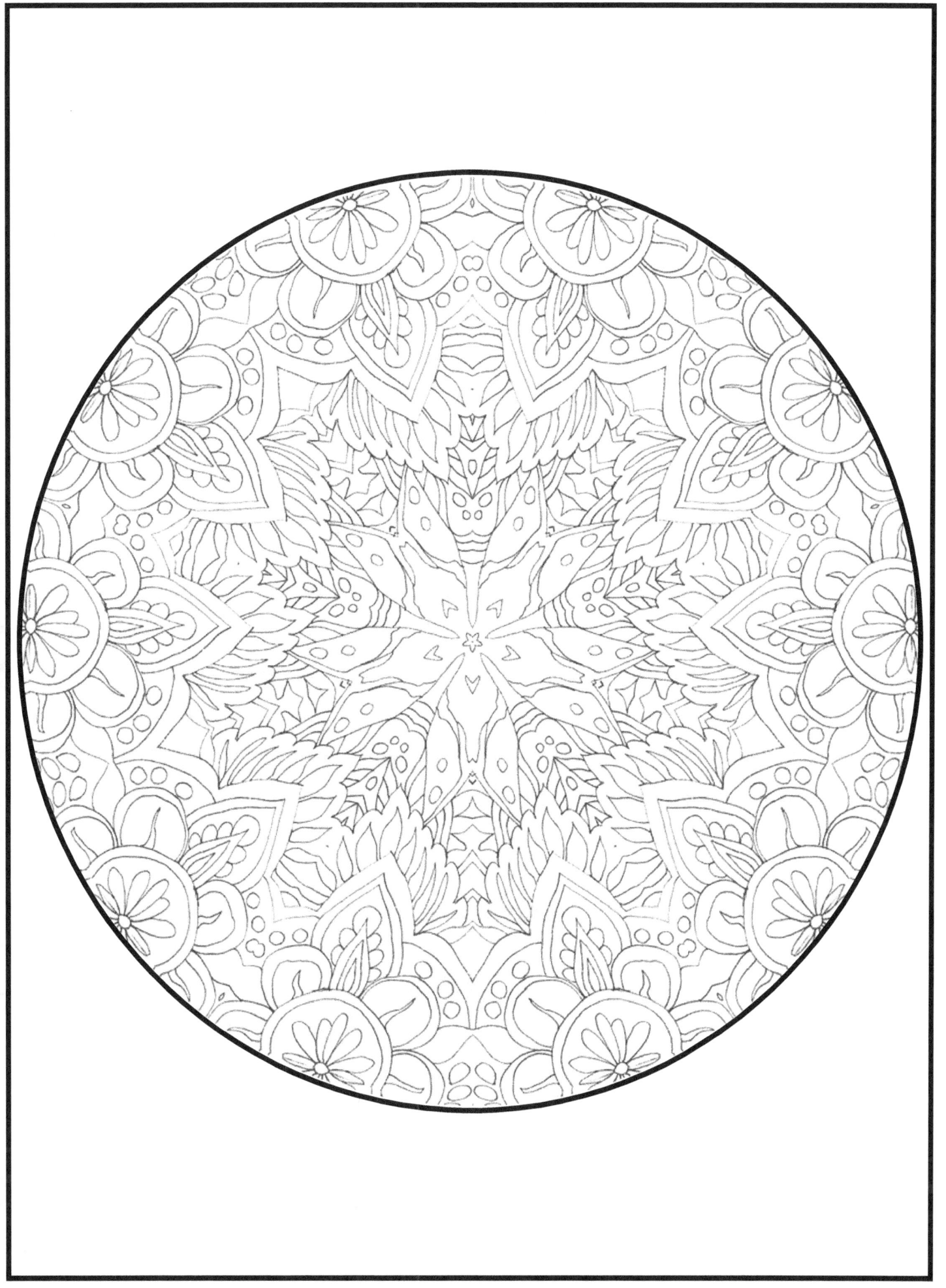

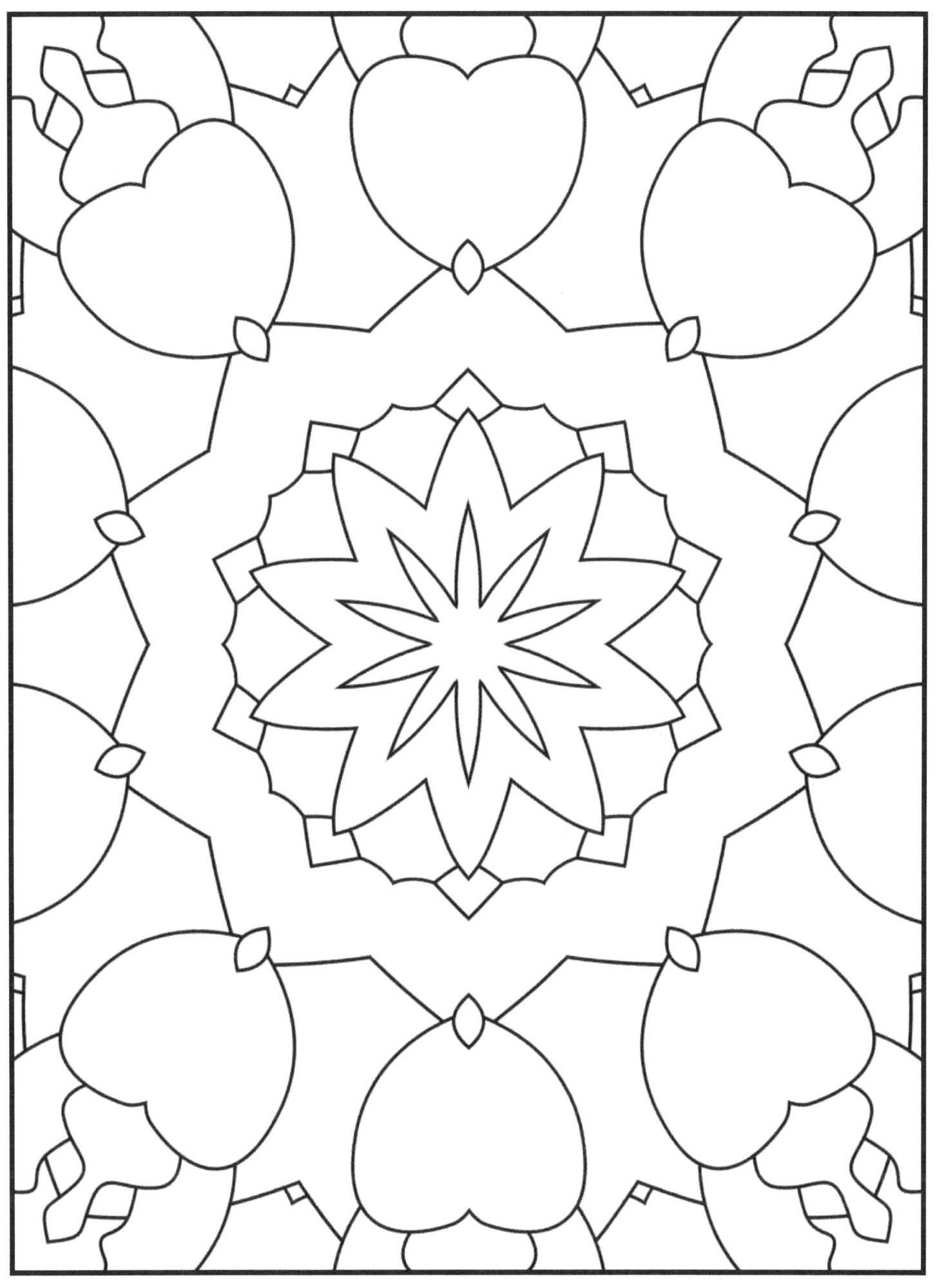

Assorted Words 1

```
Y  L  B  I  G  E  L  S  H  I  Z  C  T  S  I
R  M  I  G  S  F  S  V  E  O  A  U  B  N  N
L  O  G  F  N  L  U  Y  D  G  N  C  H  T  E
J  T  B  N  X  I  E  R  D  E  A  O  Y  U  F
B  O  V  H  I  R  Z  I  N  N  P  L  R  H  F
L  R  I  D  G  G  E  I  G  I  A  P  I  S  I
S  M  S  Z  U  I  G  S  S  H  T  R  O  S  C
O  O  E  N  O  N  E  U  A  P  T  U  D  H  I
J  U  D  D  N  W  U  N  H  H  A  T  R  D  E
O  T  K  I  S  X  R  C  T  C  C  C  X  E  N
U  H  S  I  X  P  E  N  C  E  H  J  D  E  T
R  S  J  X  G  Z  S  Y  L  P  M  A  U  A  S
N  C  I  R  C  U  M  C  I  S  E  D  U  I  X
E  X  W  R  G  E  N  T  R  A  N  C  I  N  G
D  E  G  N  U  O  R  C  S  A  T  U  K  N  O
```

AMPLY	HONORS	SILAGES
ATTACHMENT	HOPPED	SIXPENCE
CAPSIZING	INEFFICIENTS	SLEIGH
CHASER	LEGIBLY	SOJOURNED
CHUGGING	MOTORMOUTHS	VISED
CIRCUMCISED	NEIGHBOR	
ENTRANCING	RANDY	
FURNITURE	SCROUNGE	

Assorted Words 2

```
W  C  W  I  S  T  S  I  P  R  A  H  R  H  A
G  D  E  I  F  I  R  T  N  E  G  R  A  P  S
X  N  U  V  G  T  E  V  U  Y  D  T  D  A  X
P  T  I  B  J  C  S  N  V  E  D  C  I  S  P
E  R  D  L  R  P  P  T  L  B  Z  J  C  T  C
N  L  D  E  L  A  H  X  E  A  J  Y  A  E  R
E  W  X  B  T  A  W  S  L  L  R  I  L  S  O
T  H  O  Q  R  E  G  W  R  L  L  G  S  Z  U
R  L  C  E  G  K  I  U  A  E  P  U  E  S  P
A  G  N  I  L  G  R  U  G  D  I  R  M  R  I
T  G  N  I  L  L  O  R  Q  I  D  D  Q  F  N
I  A  S  B  E  S  T  O  S  S  K  L  L  J  G
O  I  B  D  E  T  S  U  G  S  I  D  E  O  Z
N  I  O  N  I  M  O  L  A  P  S  D  O  D  S
S  F  D  E  I  L  P  P  A  S  I  M  J  C  G
```

ASBESTOS	GENTRIFIED	RADICALS
CROUPING	GURGLING	ROLLING
DISGUSTED	HARPISTS	SOLDIERS
DISQUIETED	MISAPPLIED	WADDLED
ENLARGER	MULLETS	
EXHALED	PALOMINO	
EYEBALLED	PASTES	
GALLING	PENETRATIONS	

How Many Words Can You Find?

Using the letters in the game box, how many words can you create with 3 or more letters?

N	X	J	D
C	N	L	I
E	C	G	U
G	A	V	I

1	13
2	14
3	15
4	16
5	17
6	18
7	19
8	20
9	21
10	22
11	23
12	24

Puzzle #1

FIND THE NUMBERS

```
1  7  3  4  8  9  0  7  8  5  8  3  0  7  9
2  5  4  5  4  4  5  1  0  3  0  9  4  3  3
3  2  2  3  4  7  4  7  7  1  0  0  4  1  0
3  4  0  3  7  5  1  3  1  1  4  5  7  4  3
9  4  8  8  3  4  8  9  0  6  0  9  3  4  2
4  8  2  9  1  3  1  0  3  9  8  6  4  3  2
0  6  0  1  0  4  4  4  2  1  4  0  1  0  6
0  7  7  1  7  9  7  5  8  2  5  1  5  2  3
3  0  5  1  5  7  3  9  4  8  0  3  0  8  9
8  3  8  5  1  4  3  4  8  3  8  1  6  4  8
1  0  5  4  8  1  7  2  2  5  0  5  0  7  7
0  2  0  9  0  9  8  4  3  7  4  4  3  8  8
1  1  2  4  3  6  9  7  1  3  4  4  8  5  7
1  5  5  1  0  4  2  2  0  7  3  5  2  5  0
4  3  4  5  2  2  4  1  5  8  2  0  3  6  4
```

18708	584034543	54451030943
149034	4589741802	547243909843
0398643	7437414888	9703858709843
03810114	24390609843	
20909843	27147451089	

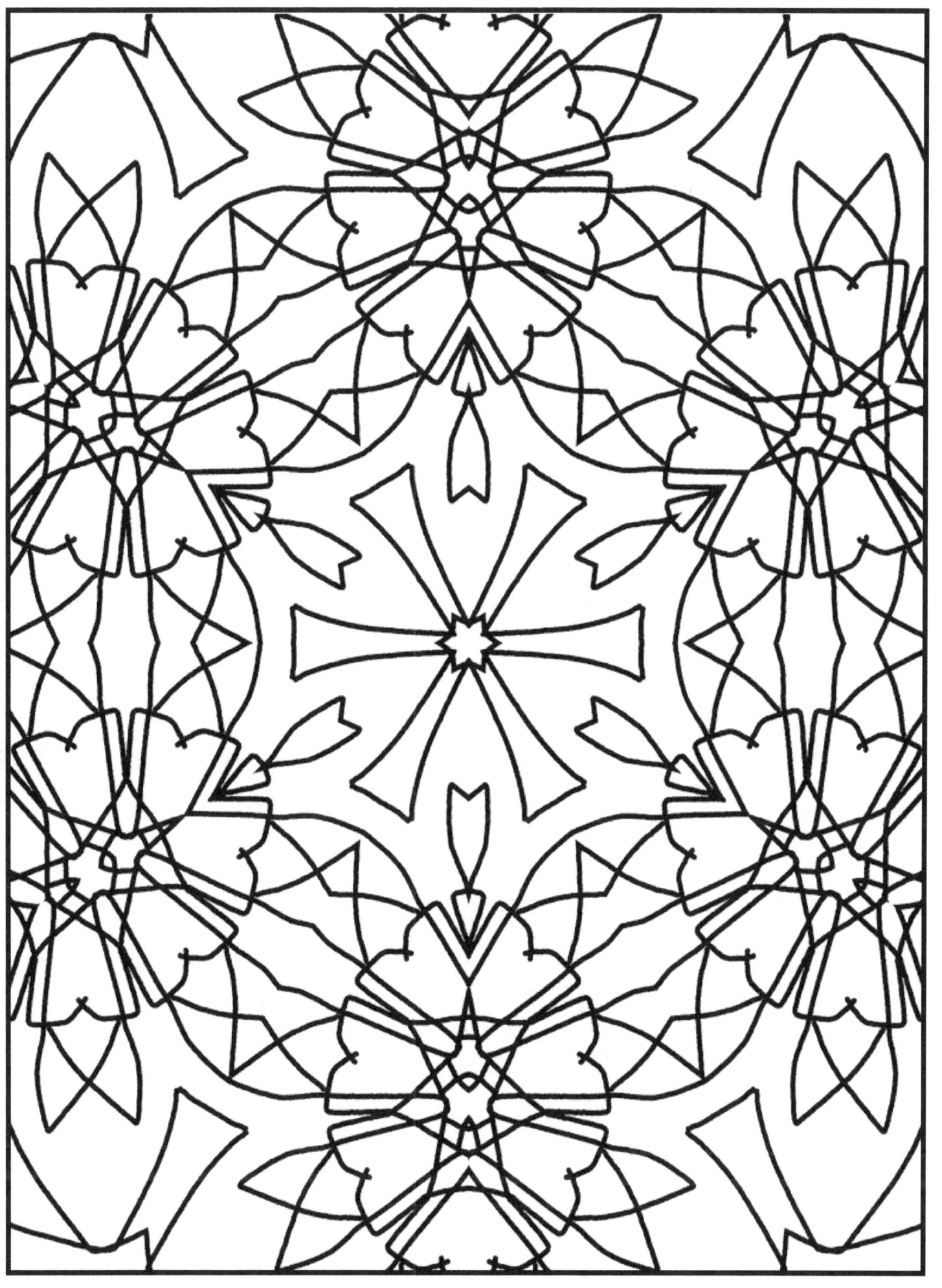

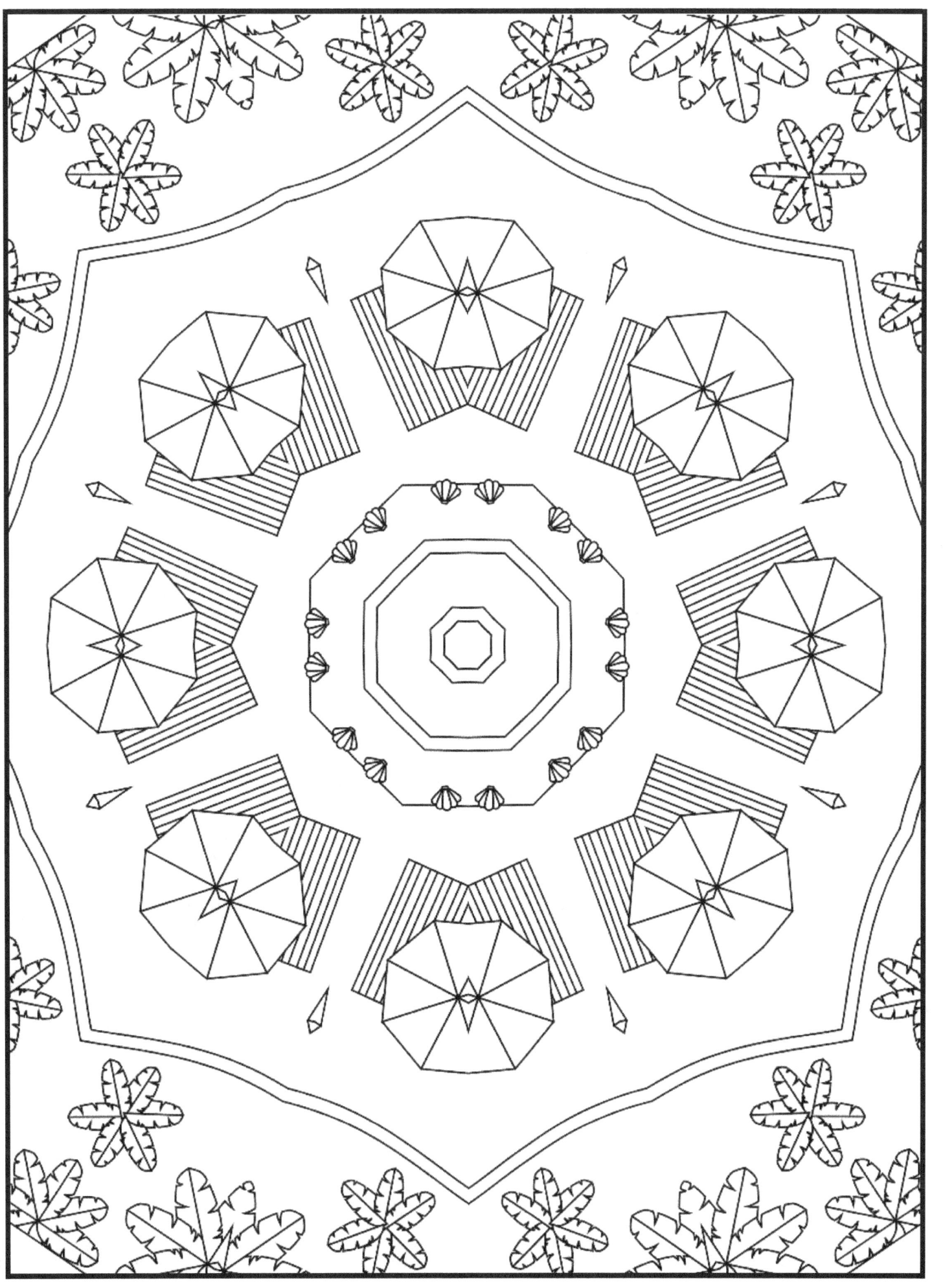

Puzzle #1
MEDIUM

6	1			9		7		
			2		1			6
		3	4			8	9	
1			7	5	3		6	9
						1	8	
4	6	5	1	8				
		6		2				
	7	8		1		2	5	
9					4			

Puzzle #2
MEDIUM

			4	1				
	7	8			6	5	4	
	4				2		7	
4					3	7		5
	8	5	1	7			2	6
	1	7	6					3
			6					9
		9		4	5		3	
7			9					

Puzzle #3
MEDIUM

			4				9	
	6	2			8			
7			5		1	3	4	
				4	6		7	
				3				
	2		9	1		6		8
9	8	5			4	7	1	3
	7	3				9	6	
			3			2	8	

Puzzle #4
MEDIUM

		3	2			4	8	
		8	6	5				9
9		4						
		9				1		
8		7	1	4				6
1	3			6			7	4
4					3		1	7
	5		7	1	9		4	8
		1				2		

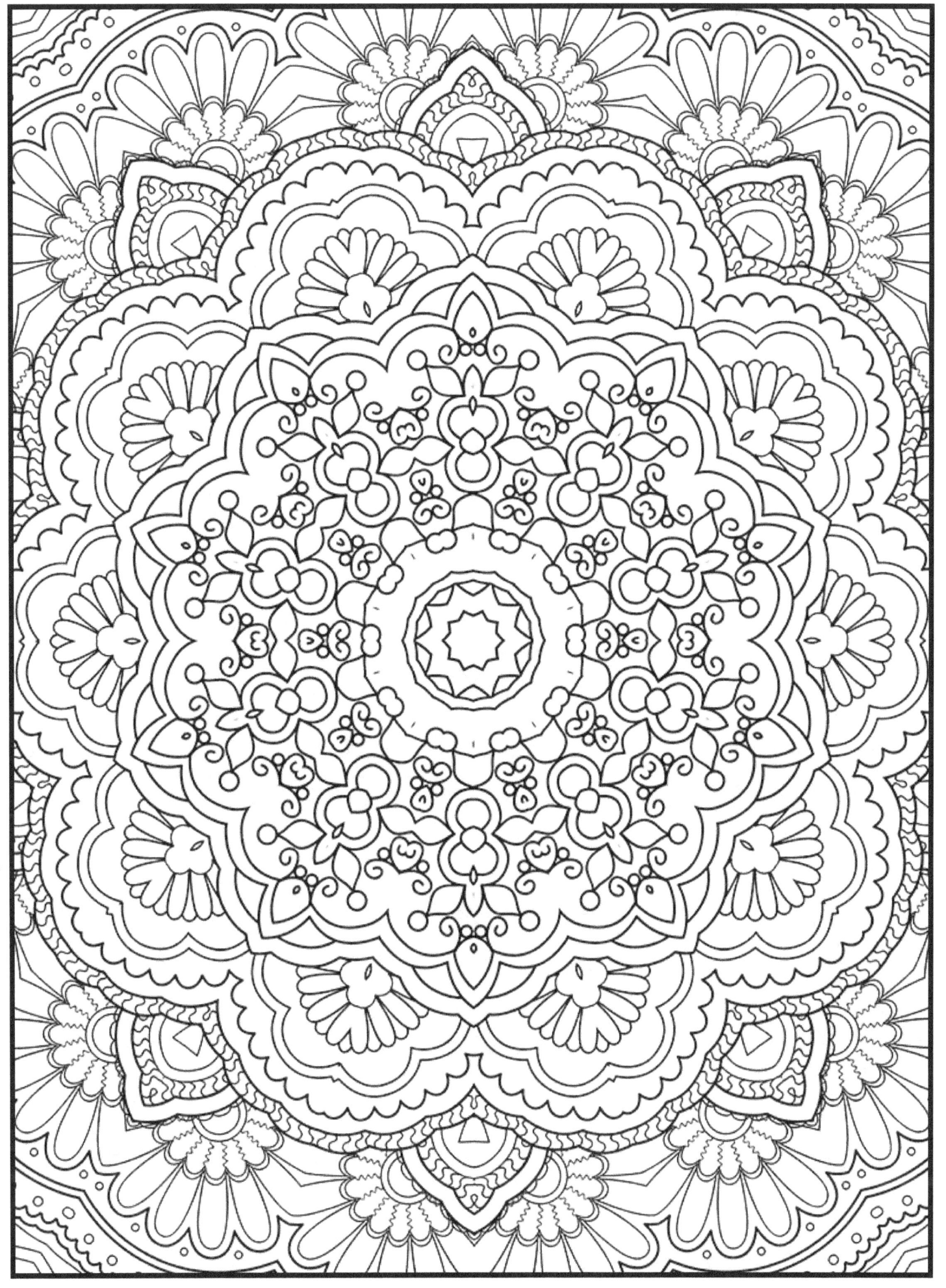

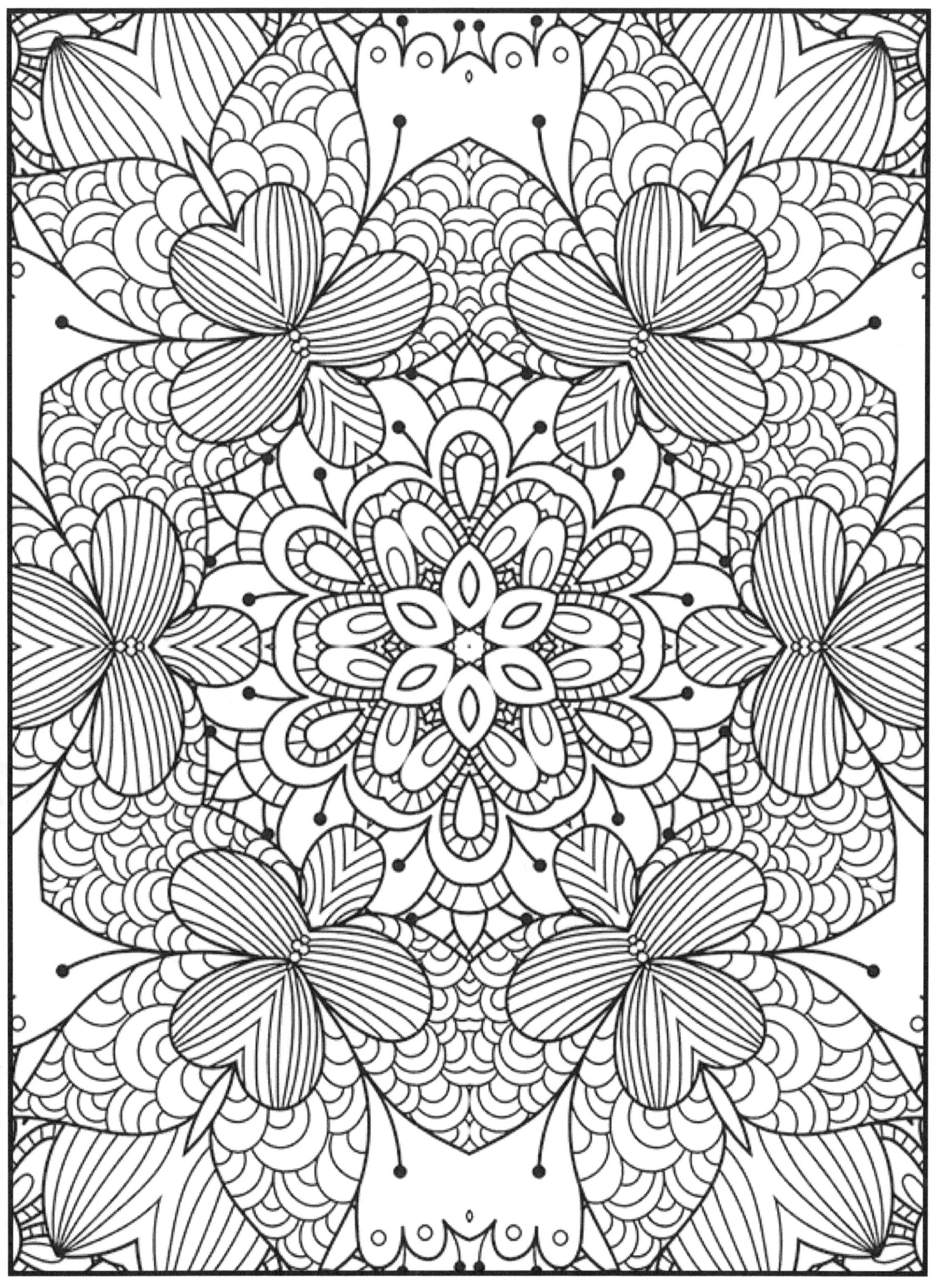

How Many Words Can You Find?

Using the letters in the game box, how many words can you create with 3 or more letters?

A	T	A	S
0	C	H	H
y	L	J	u
s	V	u	F

1	13
2	14
3	15
4	16
5	17
6	18
7	19
8	20
9	21
10	22
11	23
12	24

FIND THE NUMBERS

3	4	9	8	0	7	9	0	2	5	1	6	0	2	8
1	5	2	3	9	3	4	2	4	4	3	4	7	5	4
1	2	8	3	0	3	6	2	7	4	0	6	7	9	2
8	9	3	4	4	1	6	7	2	4	1	0	2	9	7
8	4	4	4	3	5	7	3	8	0	2	7	8	4	4
9	1	5	3	8	8	4	4	4	4	6	3	6	3	9
7	4	0	7	4	1	5	3	8	2	1	0	3	6	1
4	8	1	3	4	8	8	4	4	2	0	4	6	0	4
3	1	8	3	3	8	6	1	7	2	5	8	0	4	3
6	3	1	1	0	4	4	7	0	6	0	8	3	8	9
9	1	3	0	4	4	7	7	1	5	4	7	9	4	0
7	0	3	5	4	3	7	3	1	4	6	9	8	4	2
4	9	4	1	1	7	2	5	7	4	0	8	9	0	2
3	2	9	5	9	3	9	4	0	5	9	7	5	4	6
3	5	4	5	8	9	7	4	3	6	9	7	8	1	3

0608389	8814324	84274914
0870243	9436048	89743697
2472848	9708943	547649943
2740679	9740114	3486714078
3454324	24380243	5748471497
5740314	50181843	8974369743
8103347	67841408	
8471039	74344243	

Assorted Words 3

```
O  U  E  B  S  P  R  O  F  E  S  S  E  S  C
E  I  H  S  E  R  G  Q  Y  Q  I  G  L  O  O
A  D  S  K  R  G  E  G  Y  T  X  E  J  S  N
R  F  C  W  Y  E  R  H  N  J  U  D  E  M  S
T  L  I  C  A  C  M  A  S  I  J  X  T  O  I
H  O  Z  C  X  R  R  M  M  A  U  D  T  Y  D
L  G  B  A  I  G  C  E  I  M  W  R  I  B  E
I  G  A  U  T  O  N  O  M  Y  A  H  E  H  R
E  E  C  T  V  U  N  I  N  A  Q  R  S  P  E
S  D  K  Z  L  B  D  A  T  V  T  L  I  I  D
T  Q  D  F  D  U  D  E  D  I  E  O  N  A  D
L  E  A  D  S  U  P  E  K  O  N  R  R  Z  N
G  R  T  Y  K  I  R  R  I  N  P  G  S  I  S
R  L  E  F  O  V  A  R  Y  U  I  O  I  E  A
W  U  P  T  O  M  A  I  N  E  S  F  H  V  S
```

AFICIONADO	DUDED	JETTIES
AUTONOMY	EARTHLIEST	LEADS
BACKDATE	FINKED	OVARY
CONSIDERED	FLOGGED	PROFESSES
CONVERSES	GRAMMARIAN	PTOMAINES
CRAWS	IGLOO	RUING
CREMATORIA	IGNITING	
DISHWASHERS	IMMERSE	

FIND THE NUMBERS

```
3  1  4  2  0  1  5  4  7  9  7  4  1  4  4
7  3  8  8  3  0  1  6  6  3  6  0  8  1  1
8  5  3  5  2  8  4  0  3  3  7  8  7  9  5
8  5  1  2  9  4  4  0  3  6  2  4  3  6  8
4  9  4  4  3  4  3  5  8  7  8  7  4  2  8
4  4  0  8  3  0  3  0  4  4  0  4  2  2  3
4  9  5  4  9  7  4  0  2  2  2  9  2  6  8
8  9  0  4  7  4  7  4  5  0  9  8  9  0  9
5  3  7  9  3  3  4  8  4  3  1  0  5  3  3
0  2  4  5  4  8  8  4  4  1  8  4  4  5  1
3  4  5  4  9  8  1  5  8  4  7  1  2  4  3
0  2  5  5  2  8  3  2  9  3  0  2  0  4  9
9  1  7  3  5  4  8  5  3  5  0  3  7  0  2
3  2  7  9  7  9  7  1  6  3  5  9  4  7  5
9  9  2  5  2  4  3  9  9  4  3  9  0  3  3
```

243994	7485189	44036243
343044	7884448	89047474
443347	9440924	97451024
507455	9742443	97873304
974144	18594305	
2478785	24241020	

Puzzle #5
MEDIUM

7							6	9
5		6	1		2		4	
1	8	9	4			5		
6	2				3	9		
			9	5	4			
	5					3	7	
8	7				9	6		2
		3		7	5	8		
				1				

Puzzle #6
MEDIUM

	5	1	3					7
9			1			5		4
7						9		
4				1	6	2	9	
		2			5			
6			7	2				8
5			9	3		4	1	
	1			6		7		
			2			3	5	

Puzzle #7
MEDIUM

8	1			5				3
		5		8		7		6
		6	2	9				
		9		2	6			
	3		5	7				4
			1	3		2	5	
1	8				2		3	
			1			4	9	7
		4	7			1		

Puzzle #8
MEDIUM

3	2						5	8
	8	4			1	9		6
	5			7	8			
			5	1	6			
		7	8		2			3
				3		8	4	1
			4					9
6	3			9		4		
		9				1	3	

How Many Words Can You Find?

Using the letters in the game box, how many words can you create with 3 or more letters?

E	V	E	U
N	I	R	A
A	E	T	T
B	O	I	Y

1	13
2	14
3	15
4	16
5	17
6	18
7	19
8	20
9	21
10	22
11	23
12	24

Assorted Words 4

```
D P R E E X I S T E D O P U J
C C E X T I N G U I S H E R S
X H T I T L I N G X S I S L V
H E A N F O Y H T S E R A R A
M E A N I N G L E S S L Q Q E
P R E C T O R S P A H E P I X
R F P X D I S R U P T I N G P
I U M I N I C A M S N H A N E
C L P S E Z I L A R O M E D C
E L S W O R G R E V O R J N T
L E Y L E V I S N E T X E S A
E S F I B E R B O A R D T I N
S T E B R P E R D I T I O N T
S S R E K A E R B W A J M G L
Y A H O O D E L B B U B U O Y
```

BUBBLED	FIBERBOARD	PREEXISTED
CHANTICLEER	HEATHEN	PRICELESS
CHEERFULLEST	JAWBREAKERS	RAREST
DEMORALIZES	MEANINGLESS	RECTORS
DISRUPTING	MINICAMS	TITLING
EXPECTANTLY	OVERGROWS	YAHOO
EXTENSIVELY	PERDITION	
EXTINGUISHERS	PLEXUS	

FIND THE NUMBERS

```
9  4  7  3  3  4  2  0  8  7  4  1  9  3  3
9  7  8  6  3  8  7  5  8  9  4  7  1  0  0
8  2  2  1  2  9  0  5  7  1  4  9  2  7  9
9  1  4  0  4  7  4  1  4  8  0  9  5  5  2
1  0  2  1  3  3  0  4  3  4  5  5  8  3  1
8  0  0  4  9  4  4  1  1  3  0  1  6  3  8
9  4  8  4  7  4  1  1  2  4  5  2  5  0  5
9  4  3  8  0  4  3  4  5  9  4  1  0  4  9
1  0  6  4  1  5  1  8  7  5  4  3  1  1  4
4  0  1  2  9  6  0  8  3  2  4  3  4  1  3
7  2  8  9  8  8  1  4  4  0  9  6  2  7  4
4  7  7  4  2  4  0  2  2  3  6  0  6  2  1
2  8  3  6  4  7  1  2  5  8  4  2  3  1  5
0  9  9  3  0  7  7  0  2  0  1  9  1  4  6
2  0  5  5  0  4  4  9  9  4  1  8  1  1  4
```

74344144	3092185943	504499418114
102077039	7498578368	
309274143	9473342087	
385543403	24208361873	
422089434	24397019824	
943481474	055141148842	
1899147420	100440027890	

Assorted Words 5

```
R  P  S  J  X  Y  S  T  G  A  V  A  T  A  R
A  M  V  E  L  Y  L  D  R  A  W  T  U  O  F
D  A  U  W  S  S  L  D  I  O  Y  P  E  I  M
I  I  X  V  H  S  T  S  I  T  U  A  L  F  A
A  N  S  V  D  M  U  R  B  P  Z  P  X  S  V
T  S  Q  Y  E  F  T  B  O  A  M  E  E  A  E
E  T  B  O  U  L  D  E  R  L  P  I  O  L  R
S  R  M  J  O  I  L  F  I  E  L  D  L  L  I
D  E  C  A  P  S  K  C  A  B  D  E  P  I  C
Y  A  L  N  L  B  A  D  A  V  R  N  R  E  K
S  M  A  B  U  I  I  T  H  Y  D  D  U  D  S
V  S  F  T  O  U  G  W  O  O  L  Y  E  L  W
K  P  S  H  I  N  I  N  G  I  X  S  D  D  B
O  R  A  C  L  I  N  G  S  W  I  E  X  F  S
S  E  Z  T  A  S  R  E  N  A  S  C  E  N  T
```

AVATAR	LIMPIDLY	RENASCENT
BACKSPACED	MAINSTREAMS	SALLIED
BLUNDERBUSSES	MALIGNS	SHINING
BOULDER	MAVERICKS	STROLLER
ENNOBLE	OILFIELD	TROUPE
ERSATZES	ORACLING	WOOLY
FLAUTISTS	OUTWARDLY	
IOTAS	RADIATES	

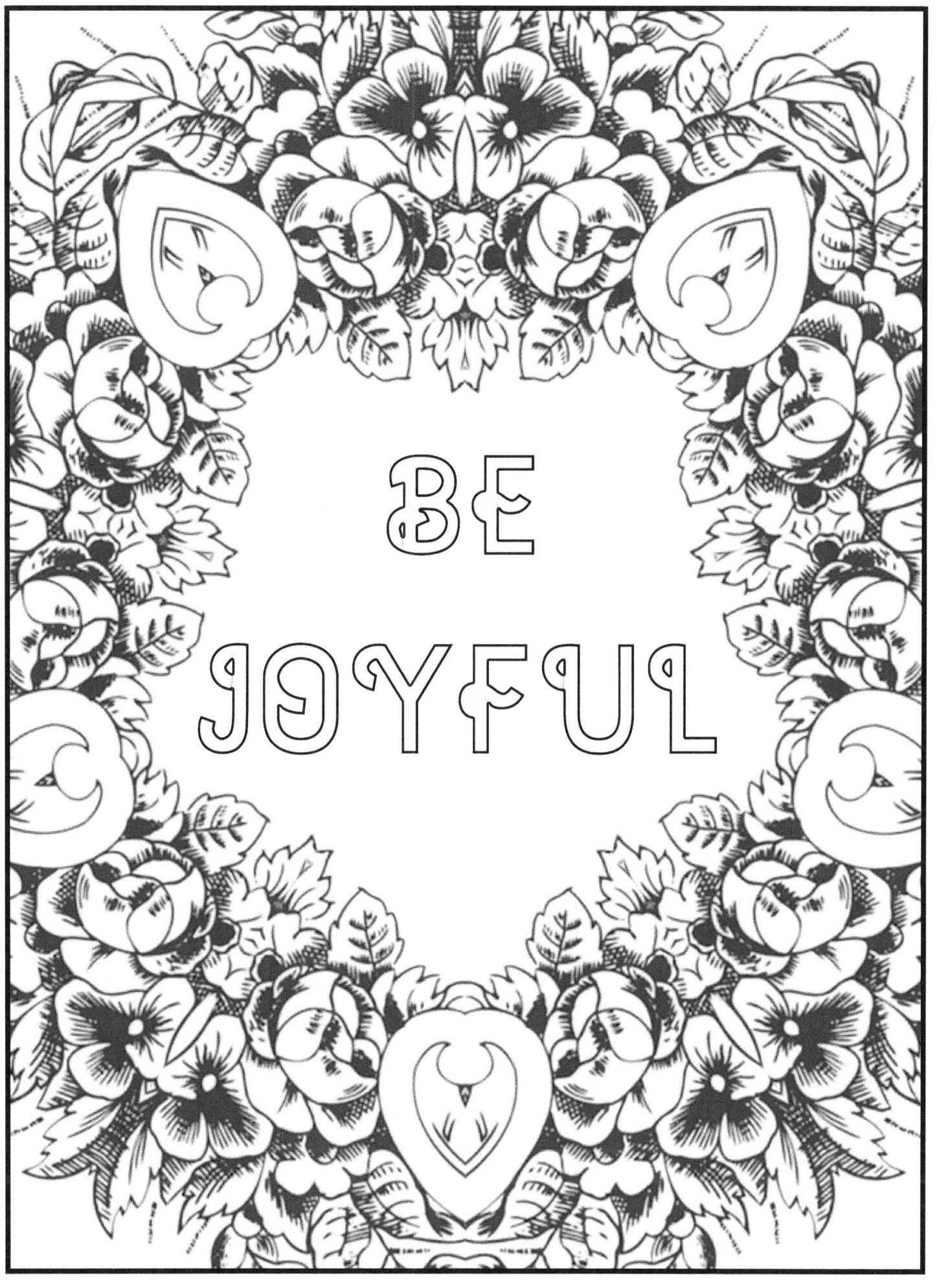

FIND THE NUMBERS

8	5	4	3	3	4	0	7	4	6	1	5	6	1	9
5	4	1	7	2	1	8	7	8	8	0	7	2	0	7
3	7	0	9	4	1	5	7	0	4	2	0	7	1	0
5	3	1	3	2	1	7	3	0	7	0	0	5	3	1
8	5	0	1	2	3	0	6	5	5	1	6	1	2	4
1	2	1	0	2	3	0	1	2	1	8	4	4	0	8
4	8	7	4	1	8	7	9	8	4	4	1	5	5	8
9	8	9	4	0	5	1	2	8	7	7	1	8	4	0
0	1	9	8	1	8	2	6	6	5	9	9	0	4	5
7	4	2	1	0	7	7	0	3	2	0	7	5	8	3
5	6	0	0	1	2	3	5	3	6	5	2	3	1	3
9	8	2	4	3	0	1	4	6	0	7	6	3	8	6
6	5	9	4	0	3	9	8	2	4	3	4	0	7	2
2	7	1	1	7	1	0	2	8	9	0	0	3	0	2
2	1	8	0	9	4	8	7	0	9	3	4	8	7	4

03210	514907	48978147
10147	546048	54541707
14108	807207	97014880
18094	2058903	98243407
18707	3009820	3481850784
98243	3014607	4784390784
203307	5433407	42107703207
208981	5814907	
482010	20184790	

Puzzle #6

FIND THE NUMBERS

```
8  2  3  3  6  4  1  9  3  4  0  6  4  7  5
0  3  3  4  8  5  8  9  3  4  3  8  1  3  1
6  8  4  4  9  8  8  3  8  9  0  1  1  4  3
3  3  4  8  9  0  3  8  9  8  4  3  9  1  5
8  9  7  6  8  9  2  4  2  7  5  1  5  7  4
8  4  5  6  2  8  7  8  2  2  0  4  2  3  7
2  6  6  2  3  0  2  8  9  8  9  1  5  8  8
0  7  4  0  4  3  5  4  5  8  8  6  0  7  4
8  0  9  0  9  2  1  6  3  4  4  2  4  4  3
8  9  9  2  0  3  4  3  4  2  4  0  8  2  3
8  8  6  3  5  5  0  8  8  4  2  8  0  9  4
4  4  1  0  2  4  8  1  7  4  9  3  8  8  1
3  3  1  0  8  9  3  4  3  8  8  4  7  4  6
8  9  1  0  8  0  4  9  1  0  1  1  6  3  9
9  9  9  3  2  6  5  7  0  2  4  2  4  7  0
```

031039064	838901143
034342408	839471842
088428094	1080491011
288243883	5746043914
342888438	8343985843
387429843	34898309843
489820943	38820888438
547843341	74883439801
570242470	83946709843

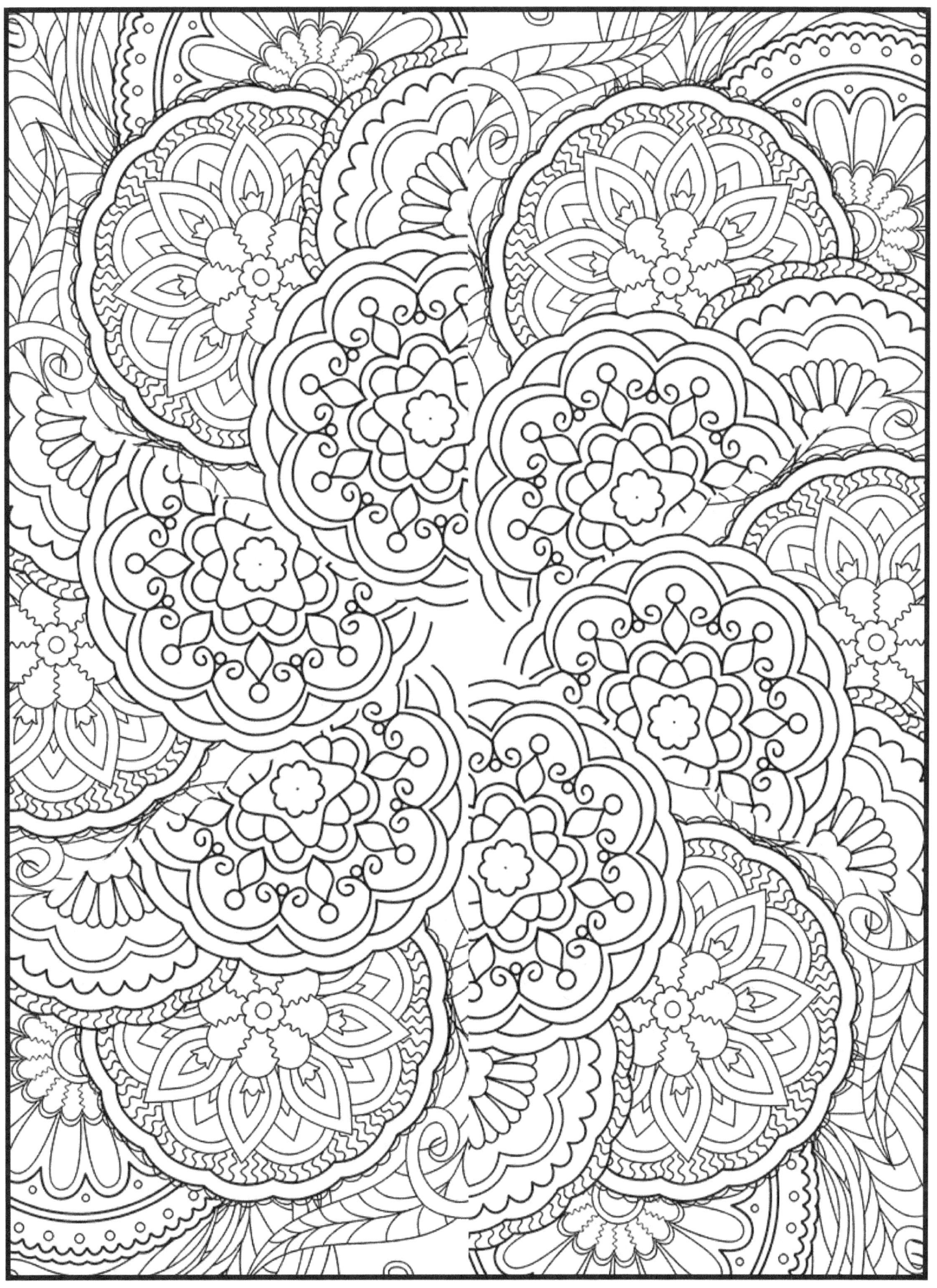

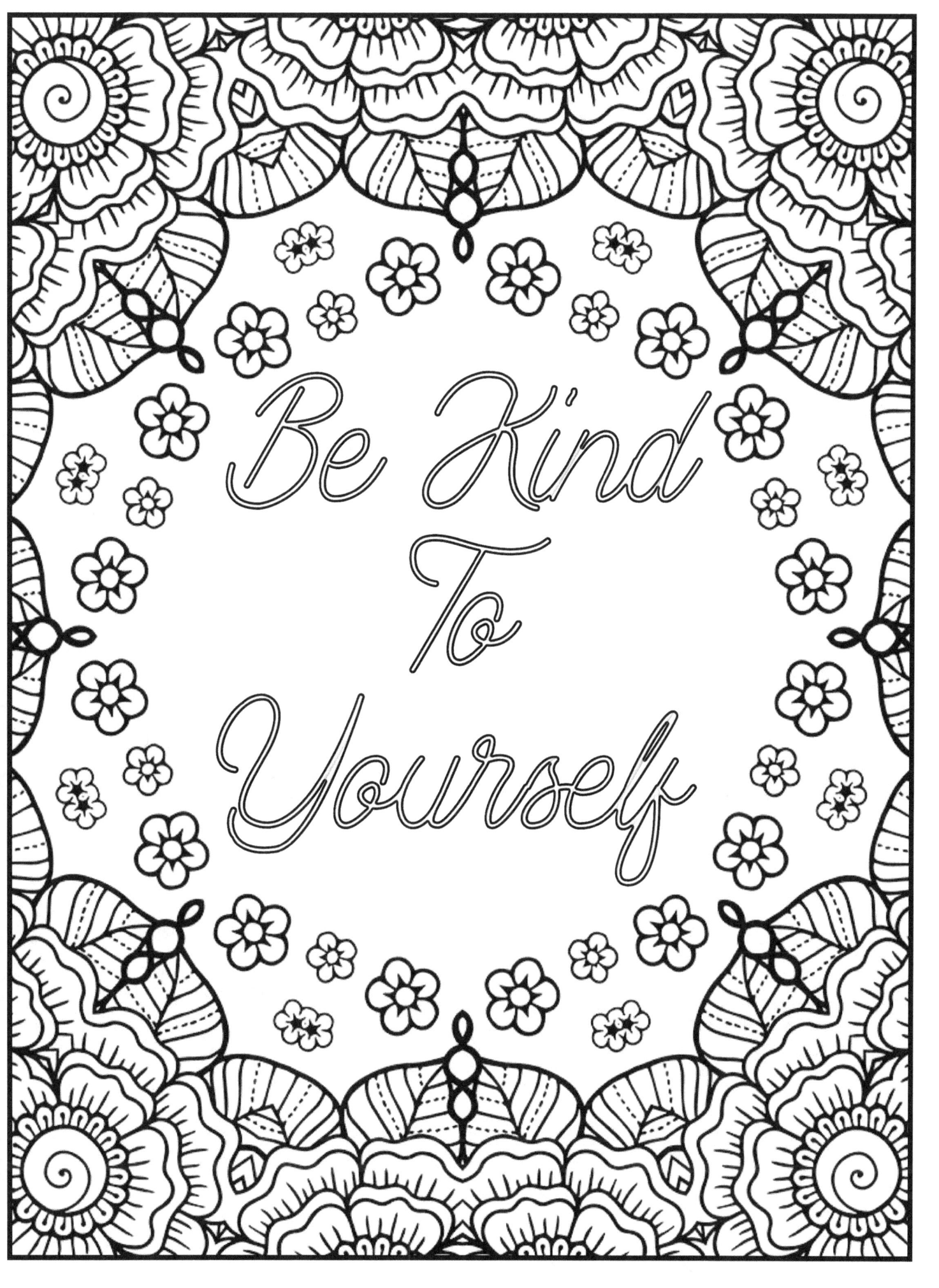

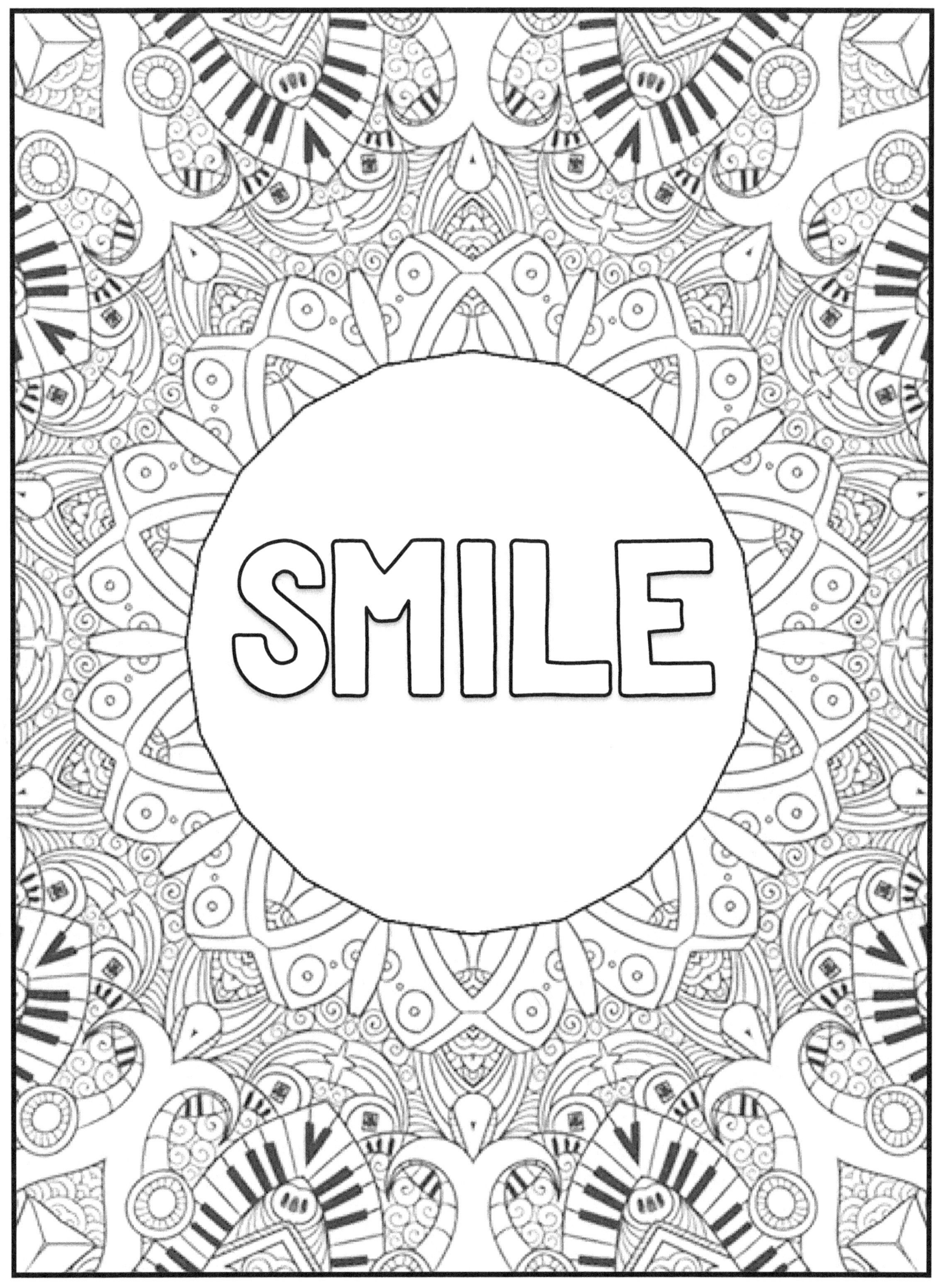

Assorted Words 6

```
R  E  P  U  B  L  I  C  M  A  Y  D  A  Y  S
S  L  W  O  R  G  K  U  M  V  A  G  I  N  A
I  N  T  E  N  D  E  D  S  K  C  I  R  T  U
A  C  O  G  H  F  E  R  S  T  R  I  D  E  I
I  O  E  I  E  F  P  F  E  E  Q  N  G  F  I
N  N  M  G  T  O  S  B  F  B  G  A  K  S  S
C  T  P  O  D  A  L  A  R  M  I  N  G  L  Y
U  R  A  X  U  E  C  O  R  E  D  N  A  I  R
L  A  P  J  U  N  L  S  G  E  D  J  D  R  I
P  V  P  G  W  F  T  S  I  I  T  L  Q  S  P
A  E  E  N  P  Y  V  A  O  F  C  O  O  J  P
T  N  D  Z  H  D  U  D  I  M  N  A  O  B  E
I  E  O  U  T  R  A  G  I  N  G  O  L  C  R
N  O  I  T  P  E  C  R  E  P  S  B  C  T  S
G  I  A  L  I  V  E  R  I  E  S  A  I  Q  H
```

ADOPT	INTENDEDS	RANGES
ALARMINGLY	KEEPS	REBINDS
BOLDER	LIVERIES	REPUBLIC
CONFISCATIONS	MAYDAYS	RIPPERS
CONTRAVENE	MOUNTAINS	SCOOTER
GEOLOGICAL	OUTRAGING	SLEDGE
GROWLS	PAPPED	STRIDE
INCULPATING	PERCEPTION	TRICKS

Assorted Words 7

```
U F O P O P U L A T I N G Y I
I M A N I A R E D R A W I N G
T N R S R R E S E M B L E S R
P S G A T O J E C B P E S P L
R E C R D I P M O S B V E U Y
O R Y D A I D V V L X I R D P
B I C W U I O I X L B A P D M
L A L D R G N I O S L T E I X
E L A C D R J E N U A H N N P
M G M W E M F N D G S A T G E
A D E D N U O T S A T N S X A
T W N B R D S S E N E S O L C
I G N I T S I X E E R P A B H
C S N O T S E C N E S B A W L
B I N O M I A L T E A S E R S
```

ABSENCES	LEVIATHANS	RADIOING
ASTOUNDED	MANIA	REDRAWING
BINOMIAL	PEACH	RESEMBLES
BLASTERS	POPULATING	SERIAL
CLOSENESS	PORNO	SERPENTS
CYCLAMEN	PREEXISTING	SNOTS
FASTIDIOUS	PROBLEMATIC	TEASERS
INGRAINED	PUDDING	

How Many Words Can You Find?

Using the letters in the game box, how many words can you create with 3 or more letters?

L	H	S	V
P	K	U	A
I	T	C	J
X	H	E	I

1	13
2	14
3	15
4	16
5	17
6	18
7	19
8	20
9	21
10	22
11	23
12	24

Assorted Words 8

```
Z  A  B  G  N  I  T  S  A  L  R  E  V  E  F
G  N  I  T  A  U  T  N  E  V  E  O  S  S  L
D  I  S  S  E  M  I  N  A  T  E  D  Q  H  A
R  F  S  C  O  L  D  I  N  G  O  E  V  O  G
E  H  T  N  L  W  B  F  E  V  V  M  D  W  O
L  G  L  A  F  S  C  A  T  F  E  Y  A  M  N
A  S  E  I  T  L  A  S  L  O  R  N  M  E  S
B  I  R  I  U  Q  I  A  D  L  L  T  A  N  O
O  N  L  Z  F  X  R  E  D  N  A  T  S  Y  B
R  K  X  F  M  E  F  B  D  A  Y  C  K  A  I
A  F  M  E  D  D  L  E  R  S  P  N  V  V  D
T  N  E  M  U  N  O  M  J  O  F  T  R  O  R
I  H  E  A  R  T  I  E  S  T  K  H  I  J  P
O  A  C  C  O  M  P  L  I  S  H  E  S  N  D
N  D  O  C  U  M  E  N  T  I  N  G  R  Z  G
```

ACCOMPLISHES	DOCUMENTING	MONUMENT
ADAPTING	ELABORATION	OVERLAY
BROKER	EVENTUATING	SALTIES
BYSTANDER	EVERLASTING	SCOLDING
CALLABLE	FLAGONS	SHOWMEN
DAIQUIRI	FLIED	
DAMASK	HEARTIEST	
DISSEMINATED	MEDDLERS	

Puzzle #9
MEDIUM

		3	5	8		7	9	4
1						5		
	9		3	2				
	3	1	8		4			6
		4		9				
	7				5			
	2	6		4	8		3	
				5		4		
5				1		9	6	7

Puzzle #10
MEDIUM

	4			5		1		
	6	5				9	3	7
8		3						4
		4				6		1
	3				6	2	8	
					5	4		
7		2	6				1	
4		6		3	9			2
	1						4	

Puzzle #11
MEDIUM

				6		1		
				4	5		2	
5			8		2	6	3	7
6			3			4	7	5
	5	4		7	6			
3				8				
1	7		4		9		6	
9			2	1				3
4		2				7		

Puzzle #12
MEDIUM

		3	1		7			2
1			4	6				9
	6		2		5			4
		4	7	1		2		
	9						7	
3							8	
4		8			2	1		
7	5		9	4				
			8				4	3

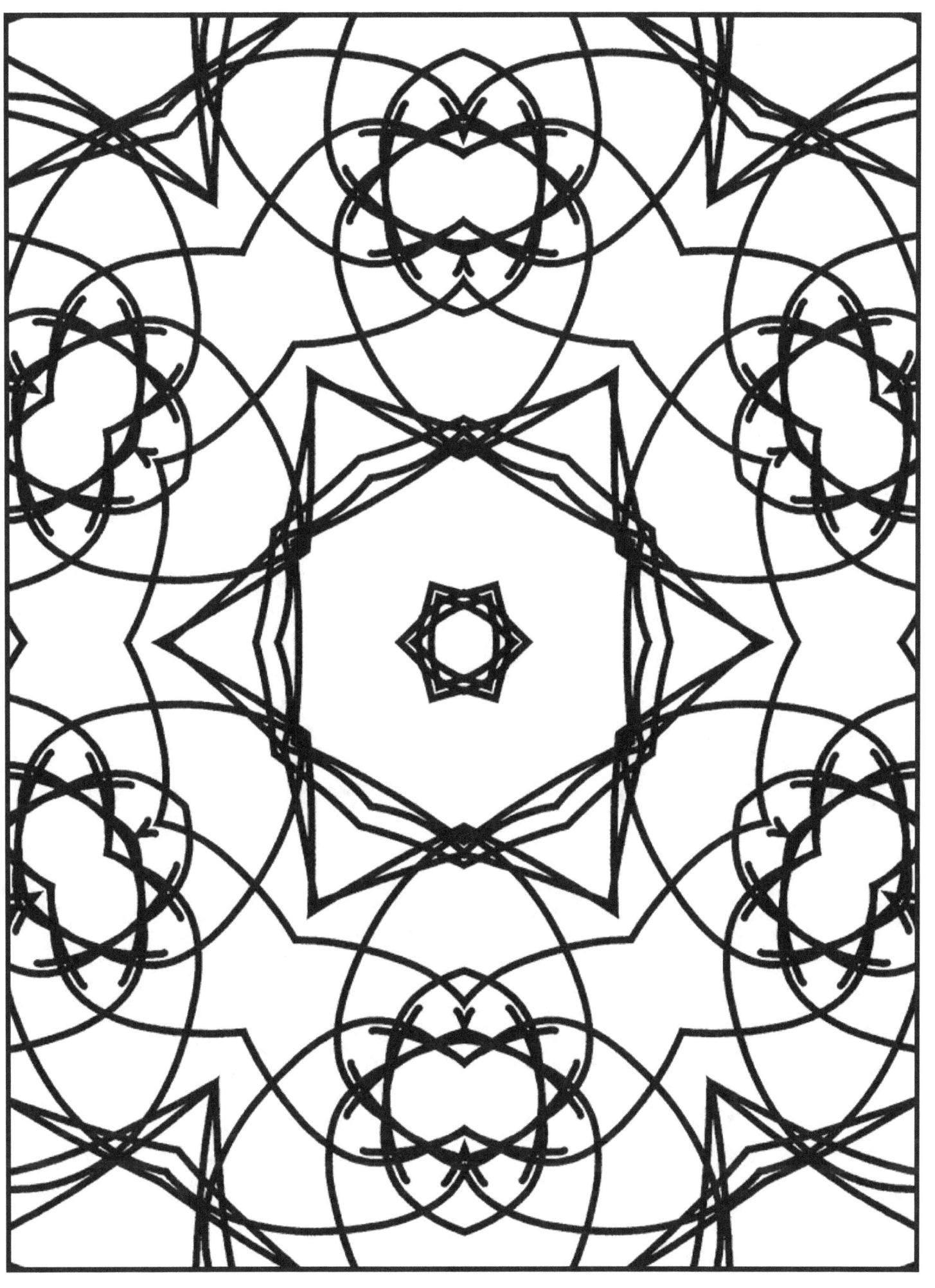

Puzzle #7

FIND THE NUMBERS

3	1	5	4	3	5	3	0	1	5	2	8	1	2	3
1	4	6	0	3	4	0	1	3	5	5	3	5	7	8
3	5	8	4	0	4	8	6	9	7	4	2	9	0	3
7	1	0	8	0	6	8	9	5	2	2	3	2	9	9
2	0	7	1	0	3	5	9	8	2	9	2	3	0	4
0	0	5	8	6	3	4	9	2	8	0	6	7	3	7
9	7	7	3	9	0	8	8	8	0	4	3	1	8	2
0	0	9	4	5	4	3	1	9	1	7	5	6	3	4
2	0	5	2	8	4	3	0	2	0	1	9	5	6	5
5	8	0	3	2	7	4	9	9	4	0	5	8	4	9
2	6	3	1	5	4	6	0	8	5	2	2	1	1	8
5	0	2	2	1	2	0	9	2	4	1	0	0	1	4
5	7	0	6	5	4	5	4	9	3	5	3	3	1	3
4	9	5	3	2	8	4	3	0	3	9	0	9	2	4
4	0	3	3	2	3	1	5	4	2	8	1	8	3	4

11895
5489349
50652036
4102009843

4554889843
5803274994
24218308843
41897029843

839472459843

Assorted Words 9

```
N  N  C  O  R  R  E  L  A  T  E  D  G  A  T
T  S  O  G  Q  S  C  I  T  C  E  L  C  E  A
D  R  T  I  N  P  I  C  N  U  G  F  G  V  N
C  Y  A  A  T  I  I  S  A  F  B  A  O  V  K
O  S  T  E  R  A  L  C  Y  P  E  I  B  X  F
N  F  G  I  H  K  L  B  K  L  I  R  L  S  U
F  R  A  N  S  G  S  U  R  A  A  T  N  A  L
E  B  Z  N  I  O  N  U  S  A  X  T  O  A  H
D  Z  E  I  T  T  M  I  M  P  G  I  A  L  L
E  N  L  E  Z  A  A  I  R  U  A  R  N  C  S
R  S  D  A  T  W  S  L  N  E  L  C  I  G  T
A  D  C  H  K  L  C  I  E  A  E  Q  N  R  T
T  R  Z  A  L  T  I  N  Z  R  K  P  V  E  D
E  Y  D  P  P  G  W  N  D  E  T  N  I  A  F
D  G  B  Y  D  E  E  R  G  V  I  S  I  N  G
```

ANIMOSITY	ENCAPSULATION	INFERNAL
BEETLING	ESCAPE	MUSKRATS
CAPITOLS	FAINTED	PEERING
CATALYSIS	FANTASIZE	PICKAXING
CLARETS	GARBLING	RELATING
CONFEDERATED	GREEDY	TANKFUL
CORRELATED	HALIBUT	VISING
ECLECTICS	HEART	

Assorted Words 10

```
L  T  C  O  N  D  U  C  T  I  V  I  T  Y  F
P  F  R  D  E  N  E  S  S  E  L  R  S  F  G
R  K  G  G  N  A  M  S  N  I  K  N  K  K  Y
A  B  G  N  I  R  E  E  N  A  C  C  U  B  P
I  J  R  D  I  S  T  I  L  L  E  D  V  B  A
S  U  S  T  C  D  Q  Z  B  F  E  L  M  S  L
I  D  Y  S  R  A  N  I  M  E  S  K  W  U  P
N  N  E  R  O  T  S  E  C  N  A  Z  C  N  A
G  S  C  T  S  T  A  U  K  O  V  D  G  B  T
N  T  F  U  S  Z  H  Y  U  O  A  T  I  O  E
J  O  P  L  B  E  W  S  K  C  O  R  C  N  D
H  U  W  W  O  A  R  H  A  N  P  B  D  N  G
E  T  M  G  W  D  T  O  Y  L  U  V  C  E  N
P  E  C  X  S  X  H  E  F  F  S  J  S  T  C
E  R  T  H  U  N  C  H  E  D  P  Z  P  S  A
```

ANCESTOR	FORESTED	SEMINARS
BEADING	HUNCHED	SLASH
BOOKENDING	INCUBATE	STOUTER
BUCCANEERING	JUNKY	SUNBONNETS
CONDUCTIVITY	KINSMAN	
CROCKS	LESSENED	
CROSSBOWS	PALPATED	
DISTILLED	PRAISING	

How Many Words Can You Find?

Using the letters in the game box, how many words can you create with 3 or more letters?

L	p	A	X
Qu	L	D	L
H	G	L	H
I	U	W	T

1		13	
2		14	
3		15	
4		16	
5		17	
6		18	
7		19	
8		20	
9		21	
10		22	
11		23	
12		24	

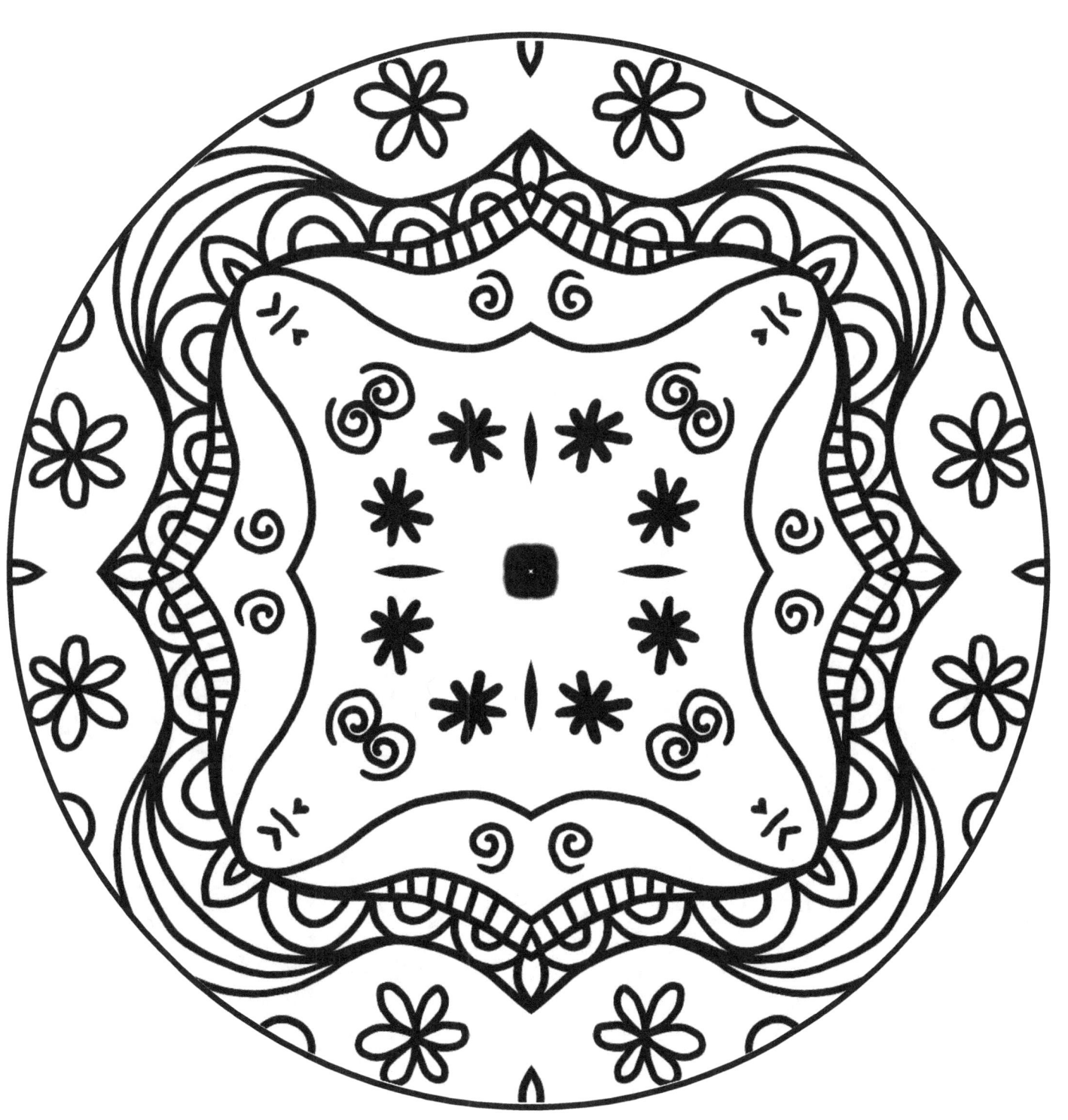

Puzzle #13
MEDIUM

```
. . 2 | . . . | . . 9
. 5 . | 2 . . | 3 . 6
. 9 3 | 4 . . | . 8 .
------+-------+------
. . 4 | 3 . . | 2 . .
. 3 . | . 1 4 | . . 5
5 . . | . 6 . | . 3 .
------+-------+------
8 . . | . 4 . | . 6 .
. . 1 | . 9 . | 8 . 7
. . 6 | 8 . 1 | . . .
```

Puzzle #14
MEDIUM

```
9 . . | . . . | . 7 .
. . 8 | . . 1 | 9 6 .
7 3 . | 4 8 . | . . 1
------+-------+------
8 5 . | . 4 6 | . 3 .
. . . | . 2 . | 1 . 5
. 7 3 | 5 . . | . . .
------+-------+------
. . 7 | 1 . 3 | . . 2
. . 9 | . . . | . 5 .
. . 2 | . . . | . 1 6
```

Puzzle #15
MEDIUM

				6	8			9
		6	5	9		2	7	
	4				2			
4	1		7	3				
3	9		8	1	5			
		8	9			3		7
2	3	1		4		8	9	
8	6			5	1			3

Puzzle #16
MEDIUM

				1	5	8	4	7
		8			3		9	2
	2			7		6	1	3
						7	6	
4			5					8
	9		4			2		
8		2	3	4				
		3	1					9
9					6		8	

FIND THE NUMBERS

7	8	6	1	9	1	2	0	9	5	9	9	3	3	7
7	8	3	9	3	5	6	0	4	0	6	4	7	3	2
5	5	8	3	3	0	4	7	4	0	0	7	8	7	5
5	1	6	5	0	8	3	2	9	0	6	0	4	0	9
5	4	4	4	9	7	7	6	0	9	9	8	2	9	4
0	0	6	1	1	0	1	4	3	3	2	5	0	2	5
7	9	8	9	8	6	2	1	3	8	3	5	6	7	2
7	5	4	6	0	0	7	8	1	0	5	8	8	4	0
2	8	9	9	8	9	1	5	1	4	2	2	9	7	9
0	8	5	4	9	9	8	4	8	4	2	7	0	4	4
7	7	1	4	1	1	4	1	1	4	2	4	0	5	7
0	8	3	8	8	0	1	3	0	4	2	4	3	6	1
8	3	0	7	8	4	7	4	1	7	1	1	0	2	0
0	6	7	4	2	7	4	5	7	6	8	0	6	4	7
5	5	7	1	0	0	3	2	6	3	4	9	9	5	4

14114	70927474	24182095887
203478	85499848	342411170338
374604	507720708	514095887836
3078474	542033894	945209471074
5025836	870047403	
7018909	4240310883	

Assorted Words 11

```
U  I  S  F  A  C  G  N  I  R  E  T  T  E  L
N  A  D  O  C  N  H  J  S  W  A  Y  L  A  Y
K  M  H  E  C  I  S  A  R  M  N  D  Y  D  J
P  O  P  Z  C  Q  R  E  N  D  A  I  C  R  U
G  N  I  R  O  R  R  T  C  G  I  E  U  U  P
B  E  C  A  U  S  E  O  N  O  I  O  L  G  U
R  Y  N  A  S  N  L  O  T  E  N  N  A  G  N
E  M  R  I  L  S  A  A  C  A  C  D  G  E  C
F  A  I  O  L  L  A  R  D  J  B  C  E  D  T
E  K  F  F  M  E  I  I  O  I  D  U  E  D  U
R  E  F  R  Z  I  F  O  L  U  R  A  C  U  A
E  R  Y  O  X  K  M  I  P  A  N  B  R  N  T
E  S  X  N  V  U  Z  E  L  E  B  D  W  O  I
S  E  G  D  O  P  E  G  D  O  H  L  S  B  N
Y  H  P  M  O  M  C  F  U  N  N  I  E  R  G
```

ASSAILABLE	GANNET	PUNCTUATING
BECAUSE	GLEAMS	REFEREES
BRIDALS	HODGEPODGES	RUGGED
CALLIOPE	INCUBATOR	RUNAROUNDS
CHANGING	LETTERING	SECONDED
COERCED	LIFELINE	WAYLAY
ECCENTRIC	MIMED	
FUNNIER	MONEYMAKERS	

Assorted Words 12

```
F  D  I  S  Q  U  A  L  I  F  Y  I  N  G  B
W  A  Y  W  A  R  D  L  Y  B  L  Y  R  V  B
U  N  N  J  M  A  T  U  R  I  T  I  E  S  D
A  A  Q  R  R  E  T  I  V  N  I  C  A  W  I
O  I  Y  Y  E  A  W  C  A  N  C  E  R  A  S
R  A  N  B  C  T  E  K  Q  A  C  H  R  S  P
I  D  B  T  G  C  L  D  P  C  N  X  J  H  A
G  S  E  T  E  N  O  U  N  L  W  H  B  T  R
I  T  U  E  N  R  I  D  A  E  X  T  W  E  A
N  Y  U  F  P  I  C  Y  E  S  O  O  H  C  T
A  O  B  R  H  E  A  O  O  X  S  Q  E  H  E
T  Z  M  K  B  M  S  U  M  V  H  A  W  S  S
I  R  W  O  S  O  Y  T  Q  S  N  X  E  A  B
N  E  T  A  I  R  T  A  P  X  E  O  D  I  O
G  O  V  E  R  N  E  S  S  E  S  H  C  T  L
```

ASSAULTER	DISQUALIFYING	ORIGINATING
BINNACLES	ENDEAR	QUAINT
CANCER	EXPATRIATE	SWASH
CHOOSEY	GOVERNESSES	TECHS
CODEX	INTERCOMS	TURBOTS
CONVOYING	INVITE	WAYWARDLY
DEEPEST	MATURITIES	WHEWED
DISPARATES	NAIADS	

Assorted Words 13

```
P  C  N  C  S  F  S  E  C  A  L  P  S  I  M
R  L  U  R  X  T  R  Y  P  A  C  K  E  R  W
E  X  C  A  V  A  T  I  O  N  S  F  X  S  E
A  R  R  F  Y  L  S  E  L  B  M  U  T  S  E
C  E  E  T  T  T  S  F  N  D  E  N  O  H  I
H  U  W  S  R  S  S  L  S  E  T  M  I  U  N
E  N  A  M  O  W  R  E  D  L  A  D  O  K  G
R  I  R  A  P  G  P  E  I  T  A  T  K  H  R
S  O  D  N  I  Y  B  I  E  Z  E  U  L  O  E
K  N  S  S  E  O  N  H  N  O  E  S  Y  O
Z  S  O  H  M  T  O  G  U  I  A  O  L  A  C
C  J  D  I  S  A  S  T  E  R  F  C  B  S  C
G  O  F  P  C  N  E  M  S  S  E  H  C  G  U
T  P  A  N  T  A  L  O  O  N  S  X  G  U  R
I  N  S  T  R  U  M  E  N  T  I  N  G  F  B
```

ALDERWOMAN	FLEEING	PREACHERS
BOOZIEST	HOMEBOYS	REOCCUR
BUCCANEERS	HONED	REUNIONS
CASUALS	INSTRUMENTING	REWARDS
CHESSMEN	MISPLACES	SLEET
CRAFTSMANSHIP	NEATLY	STUMBLES
DISASTER	PACKER	TROPISMS
EXCAVATIONS	PANTALOONS	WEEING

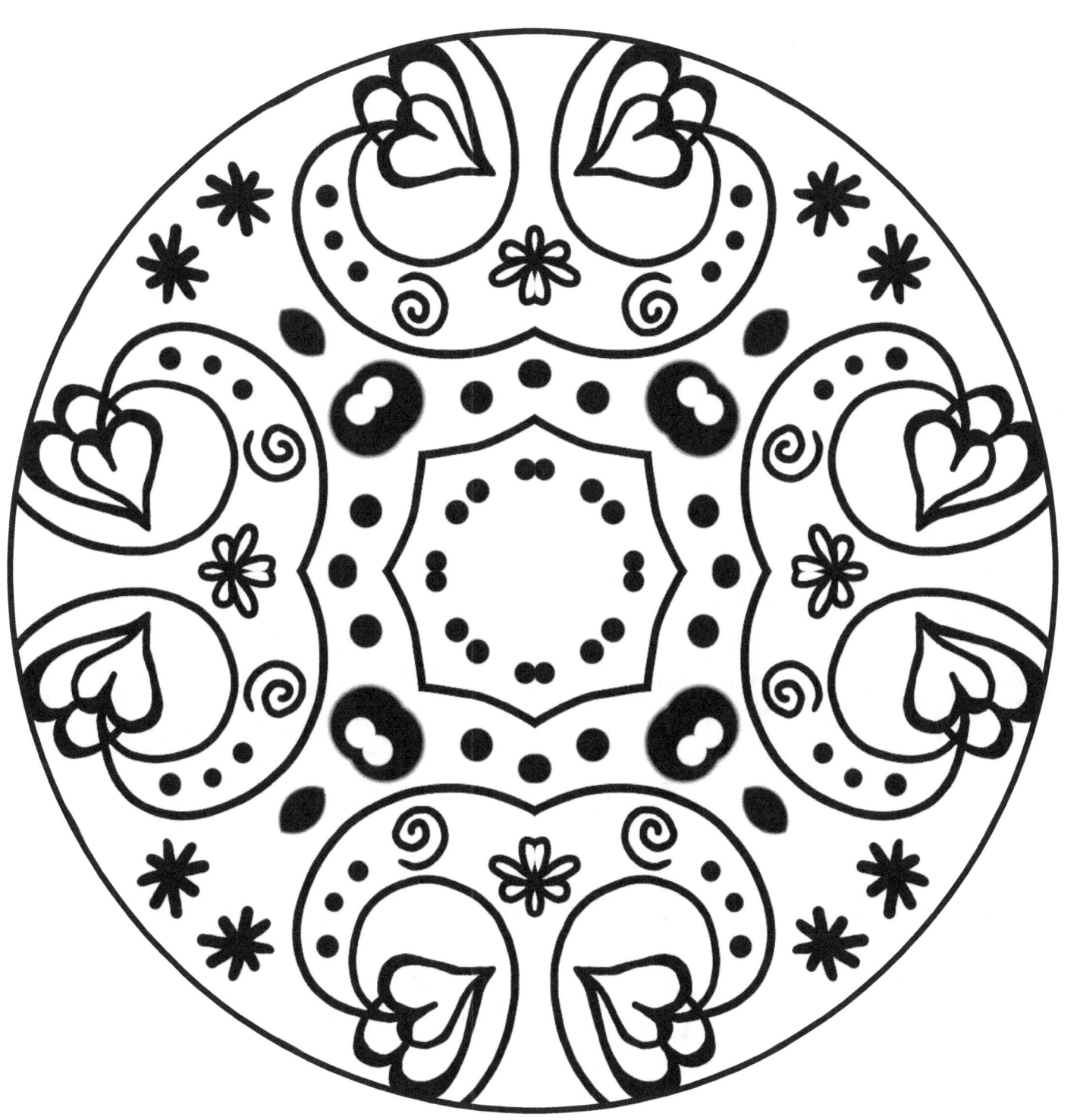

Assorted Words 14

```
S  E  I  F  I  S  L  A  F  J  D  M  Z  M  W
D  B  P  T  A  N  N  E  S  T  Q  Q  I  C  U
T  U  F  L  H  C  T  A  P  S  I  D  Y  M  I
S  T  Y  N  E  S  T  E  P  M  U  R  T  S  C
R  T  G  S  O  C  P  Q  J  U  N  M  Y  M  M
P  O  A  T  N  R  T  U  S  A  N  D  I  E  R
R  C  T  E  R  O  T  R  R  J  A  P  I  N  G
O  K  D  C  L  O  O  H  U  I  K  Z  F  D  G
J  S  Q  F  E  C  T  L  E  M  O  I  P  A  U
E  O  E  S  V  T  H  A  A  R  K  U  W  C  T
C  S  U  D  S  B  E  B  D  S  N  K  S  I  T
T  Q  V  X  U  A  Y  D  F  E  A  E  N  O  E
O  P  B  H  E  L  T  B  Q  R  R  L  R  U  R
R  S  O  M  N  O  L  E  N  C  E  P  F  S  S
S  X  G  O  U  R  M  A  N  D  S  P  F  M  H
```

ALLUDES	GUTTERS	SANDIER
ASSUMING	JAPING	SOMNOLENCE
BUTTOCKS	MENDACIOUS	SPURIOUS
CLEATS	NORTHERNERS	STRUMPETS
DETECTOR	PLECTRUM	TANNEST
DISPATCH	PREDATOR	
FALSIFIES	PROJECTORS	
GOURMANDS	SALOONS	

Assorted Words 15

```
D Z A Y E P Z S L R G U H P M
I T S E T Z A M P U L S S E H
B D S E S I I E R J U J S R P
C K E E N T R R H H T C Z S A
N W R Z L I A A E C E C J E U
Q V T P I B G O L P N W Q V P
Y F W Q E H G I B U U M B E E
C I T P Y R C L R R N A D R R
K O W J S P O E Q O O A P E I
D E R E B O S W T N B T R D Z
S C O R N F U L S A E A O G E
A K I M P A C T V R C Z D M S
X Z D E P I N S I S O N P Y H
K Z P A N D E R I N G F I K Y
I N A P P R O P R I A T E F Q
```

ABORIGINES	GLUTEN	PAUPERIZES
AMPULS	GRANULARITY	PERSEVERED
ASSERT	HYPNOSIS	SCORNFUL
BLEST	IMPACT	SNIPED
CATECHIZED	INAPPROPRIATE	SOBERED
CHEAP	MOTORBOATS	
CRYPTIC	PANDERING	
FORSWORE	PAUPERIZE	

Assorted Words 16

```
C  I  R  O  M  O  H  P  O  S  T  Z  S  N  G
S  N  S  L  S  L  I  N  K  A  G  E  S  S  A
M  S  T  N  A  T  L  U  S  N  O  C  N  E  S
X  O  X  T  O  H  I  G  H  B  A  L  L  T  D
Y  C  A  L  C  I  T  E  B  S  W  H  F  V  S
Y  R  R  R  G  S  T  O  S  T  Y  C  T  K  A
M  E  O  R  E  N  R  A  Y  P  S  E  U  L  C
T  G  L  T  E  S  I  E  I  F  M  Y  B  Q  I
T  R  V  L  P  I  E  L  G  C  I  A  D  O  D
M  P  I  U  A  M  K  R  D  A  O  V  T  P  I
A  I  D  U  O  V  E  O  V  D  R  S  I  S  F
D  I  W  H  Q  U  O  R  M  E  E  O  S  V  Y
P  I  G  G  I  S  H  N  E  S  S  M  F  A  I
V  D  S  E  T  A  I  D  U  P  E  R  R  U  N
X  J  R  A  C  Q  U  E  T  B  A  L  L  S  G
```

ACIDIFYING	MEDDLING	SOPHOMORIC
ASSOCIATIONS	OBEYS	SQUIRT
CALCITE	PEREMPTORY	STAMPS
CLUES	PIGGISHNESS	TENTS
CONSULTANTS	RACQUETBALLS	VALLEY
FORAGERS	REPUDIATES	VIVIFY
HIGHBALL	RESERVES	
LINKAGES	SMOKIER	

Assorted Words 17

```
Z  N  S  R  E  E  D  L  L  I  K  N  B  W  C
F  Z  L  G  X  F  H  E  P  O  C  H  S  W  K
I  J  Y  E  M  B  V  Y  N  O  H  P  X  S  F
M  T  S  L  A  R  R  O  C  I  S  F  C  N  Y
Q  T  S  E  L  G  L  A  X  I  A  L  O  P  S
E  E  S  E  T  R  U  L  S  A  U  T  R  V  S
T  X  C  E  N  U  S  E  A  H  L  Y  R  Z  W
G  B  U  R  I  E  C  T  S  B  E  Z  E  U  X
T  L  F  D  F  N  E  E  A  I  E  S  C  P  C
H  E  I  Y  E  S  N  R  X  E  W  R  T  L  Q
F  Y  L  B  U  S  Z  U  G  E  R  Q  I  Z  T
I  N  M  U  B  T  K  V  F  S  O  T  O  F  T
G  V  I  S  A  E  G  C  O  W  H  A  N  D  S
H  V  E  V  V  P  S  A  U  V  Y  B  A  E  Z
T  N  R  Y  K  V  E  T  U  D  W  Q  L  Z  Q
```

AXIAL	EPAULET	GREENEST
BRASHEST	EPOCHS	KILLDEERS
CORRALS	EXECUTES	LEAGUES
CORRECTIONAL	EXUDES	PHONY
COWHANDS	FILMIER	
CURTAINED	FIREBALL	
DUCKS	FUNNIEST	
ENTREATS	GLIBBEST	

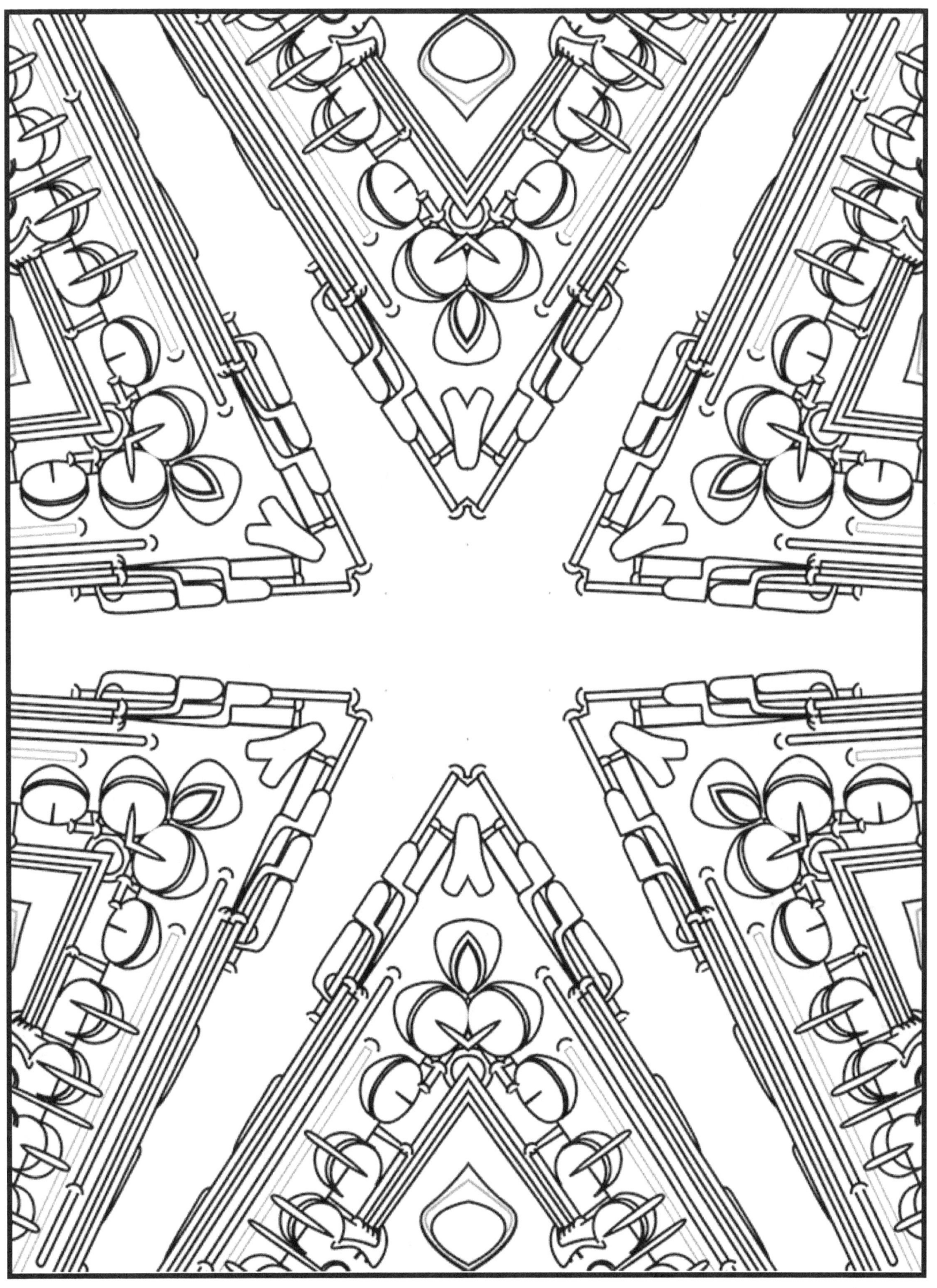

Assorted Words 18

```
J  F  W  Y  T  D  E  K  C  I  S  N  I  C  Z
B  Y  R  R  R  S  E  D  S  P  A  R  T  O  S
C  U  P  B  E  O  I  T  E  P  R  H  S  N  U
S  A  B  A  R  G  T  G  I  T  U  I  S  D  N
O  E  T  U  R  A  G  A  O  M  A  S  V  O  L
M  U  I  S  F  E  I  A  M  L  I  L  S  N  E
B  R  O  T  R  F  H  N  B  A  O  L  S  E  S
R  H  E  U  I  E  E  T  I  T  L  I  U  D  S
E  G  S  G  I  S  T  R  O  N  E  C  D  P  R
R  X  H  G  N  T  R  A  S  M  G  P  X  A  Z
O  B  N  C  O  A  T  E  R  O  E  K  R  E  R
R  R  R  C  K  O  M  C  V  C  X  H  G  A  S
L  P  H  O  N  I  E  R  Y  D  L  C  C  D  C
T  H  G  I  E  W  R  E  H  T  A  E  F  C  J
S  N  O  I  T  C  U  R  T  S  N  I  H  J  E
```

ADVERSITIES
BRAINING
BUFFERS
CARPETBAGGER
CHEMOTHERAPY
COATER
CONDONED
CRATERS

EXCLAMATORY
FEATHERWEIGHT
INSTRUCTIONS
LIMITED
MANGER
PHONIER
PUSSES
RADIOLOGIST

SICKED
SLATED
SOMBRERO
SUNLESS
TRAPS

Assorted Words 19

```
H  P  S  C  O  E  X  I  S  T  S  G  K  A  S
A  H  N  G  L  K  F  E  R  R  E  T  I  N  G
Y  I  P  O  N  A  R  Z  U  C  R  V  P  W  L
M  L  E  V  S  I  P  U  D  E  I  R  R  A  M
I  O  R  E  E  R  R  B  E  R  I  L  R  I  O
N  S  J  R  I  L  U  E  O  T  N  A  E  M  D
O  O  U  R  S  L  B  K  D  A  U  K  B  B  U
R  P  R  I  L  D  E  A  A  I  R  A  I  V  L
I  H  E  D  K  E  N  L  N  S  D  H  T  A
T  E  R  D  R  U  D  A  C  E  E  N  E  X  T
I  R  S  E  K  H  F  Q  H  R  I  K  O  D  I
E  N  Y  N  W  A  R  P  O  K  U  L  N  C  N
S  E  Z  I  T  A  M  A  R  D  C  L  A  U  G
P  E  N  T  H  U  S  E  S  T  E  E  U  Z  S
V  F  D  G  N  I  T  I  R  E  M  E  D  A  A
```

ALIENABLE
ANCHORS
CERTAINER
CLAPBOARDED
COEXISTS
CONSIDERINGS
DECKHANDS
DEMERITING

DRAMATIZES
ENTHUSES
FERRETING
HAUTEUR
MARRIED
MEANT
MINORITIES
MODULATING

OVERRIDDEN
PERJURERS
PHILOSOPHER
PRAWN
SUNKEN

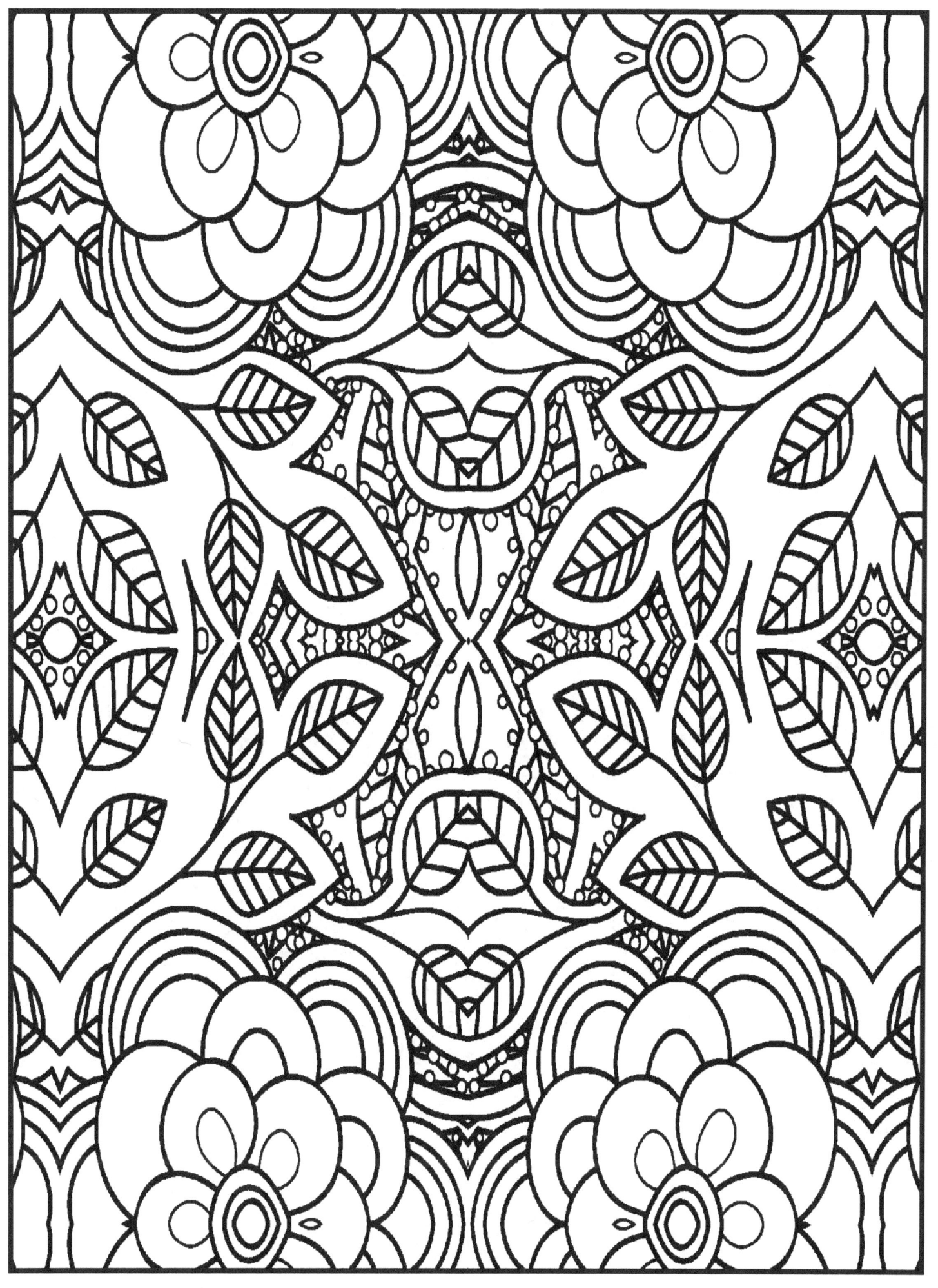

Assorted Words 20

```
F Y D L Y S E N I R E C Y L G
O V U U I C H A N G E O V E R
T C R D X R X S R E L W O R P
R N O O O L A X Y W A I S T H
S E I L B M E S S A L J W B Y
Y I D Y O S A A S O R E S E P
W G V R H N F I L L R F W S E
I H Y A O T I L N U E P F D R
Y I N E L B D Z U S B H V A B
P N G J X E I I E T A I A M O
Y G V W F H N C W L T B F E L
G E R M I N A T E D I E C S I
B X P E B U L L I E N T R H C
D E T C U D N I E N G A E E C
C H E C K B O O K D E S B S D
```

AFFRAYS	EBULLIENT	LIRAS
ASSEMBLIES	EXHALED	MESHES
BANDWIDTH	FIBULAE	NEIGHING
BORDER	FLUTTERED	PROWL
CHANGEOVER	GERMINATE	REBATING
CHECKBOOK	GLYCERINE	SORES
COLONIZE	HYPERBOLIC	VALENTINE
DOMAINS	INDUCTED	WAIST

Puzzle #17
MEDIUM

	6	1	9	3			2	7
					4		3	5
8			7	6				
	2					9		
		4		2				
		3	5	7	8		6	
5				8		3		
			1	9		5		
	4	9	2			1		

Puzzle #18
MEDIUM

3	4			8				
7	6				1			9
2		5						1
				9				2
6		2				5	9	
		4			5	3		
1		7		4	2			8
					9	7		
8			1	7			6	4

MEDIUM

		7	4	3			2	8
3	8			5		6		
2	5							7
	3			6		7		1
5			9	8		3		2
7	6				3			
				4	2			
4	2							5
		9	8		5		4	

Puzzle #20

MEDIUM

	9				8	3		
1			7	4			5	
5	6	8		9	2			1
2			8		5		1	
6	1				9			2
		4						
							7	
	7	6	1	2	3		8	
8						1	6	

How Many Words Can You Find?

Using the letters in the game box, how many words can you create with 3 or more letters?

L	C	I	I
L	E	A	F
X	T	E	s
A	E	u	I

1	13
2	14
3	15
4	16
5	17
6	18
7	19
8	20
9	21
10	22
11	23
12	24

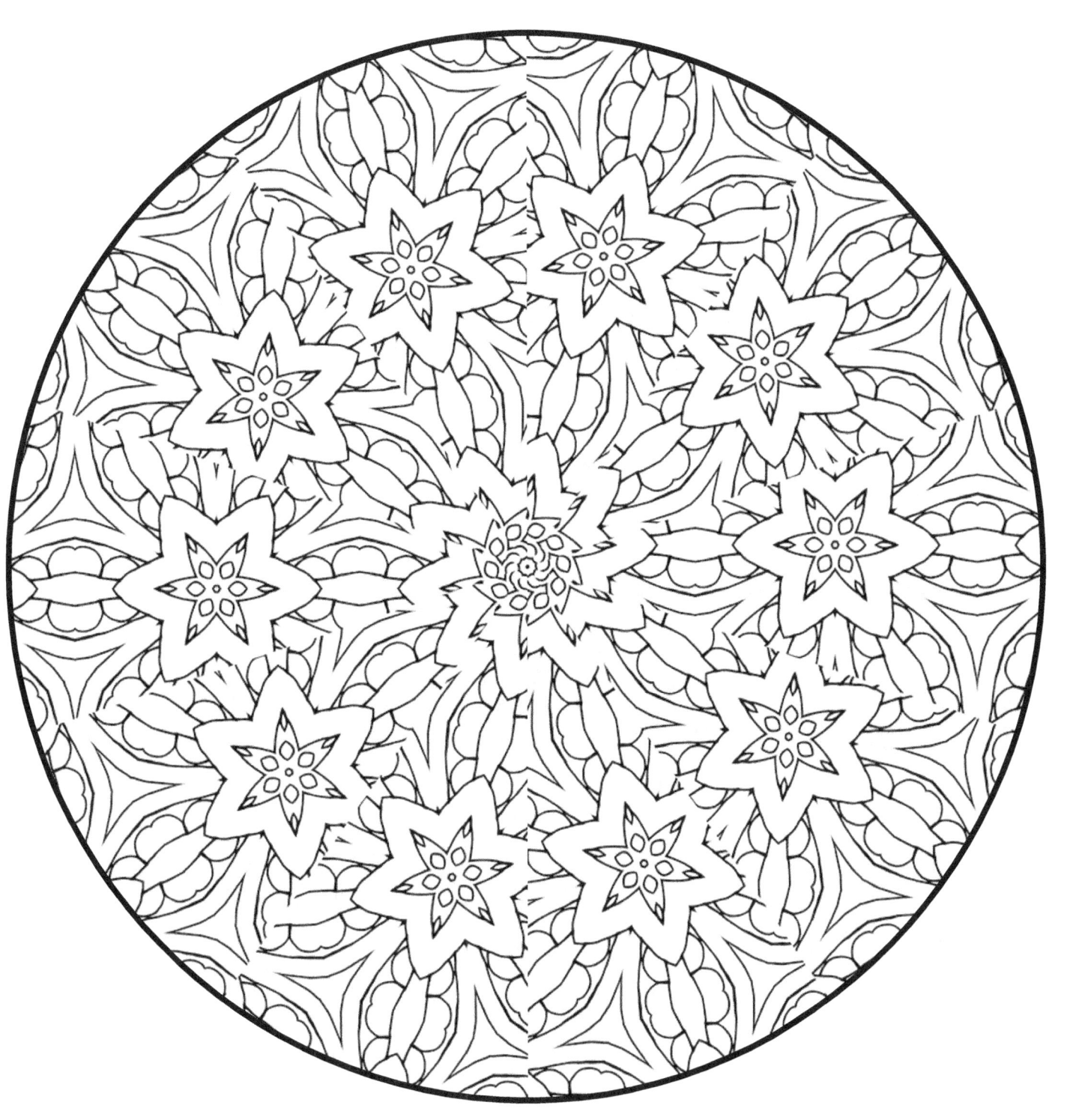

Solutions

Number Search Solutions

FIND THE NUMBERS
Puzzle # 1

```
  7 3 4 8 9 0 7 8 5 8 3 0 7 9
    4 5 4 4 5 1 0 3 0 9 4 3
3 2   3     4
  4 0   7       3
9   8 8 3 4 8 9 0 6 0 9 3 4 2
  8   9 1 3 1 0 3 9 8 6 4 3
    0   0 4 4 4       4
0       1   9 7 5 8       1
3       5     3 9 4 8
8         4     4 8 3 8
1           1 7   2 5 0
0 2 0 9 0 9 8 4 3 7 4 4
1             7 1   4   8
1             0 7   5   5
4                 8 2
```

FIND THE NUMBERS
Puzzle # 2

```
3 4 9 8 0 7 9     2             8
  2 3     3 4 2 4 4 3 4 7       4
    3 0   6 2 7 4 0 6 7 9 2
    3     4 1   7 2         9 7
8     4     5 7 3 8         4 4
9 1 5 3 8     4 4 4 4       3 9
7 4 0 7 4 1 5 3 8 2 1       6 1
4 8 1 3 4 8 8 4 4     0 4   0 4
3 1 8 3 3 8 6 1 7 2     8 0 4
6   1 1 0 4 4 7 0 6 0 8 3 8 9
9     0 4 4 7 7 1 5 4 7   4
7       4 3 7   1 4   9 8     2
4         7 2 5   4 0   9 0
3           9 4     9 7   4
          8 9 7 4 3 6 9 7 8   3
```

FIND THE NUMBERS
Puzzle # 3

```
  1 4 2 0 1 5 4 7 9 7 4 1 4 4
7   8
8     5       4 0 3 3 7 8 7 9
8       9 4 4 0 3 6 2 4 3
4           4 3 5 8 7 8 7 4 2
4               3 0 4
4   5           4 0 2 2
8 9 0 4 7 4 7 4 5 0 9
  3 7                 1 0
    4               4   4 4
    5 4 9 8 1 5 8 4 7     2 4
    5   2             0       4 9
        4                 3     2
          7                 4
        2 4 3 9 9 4           3
```

FIND THE NUMBERS
Puzzle # 4

```
9 4 7 3 3 4 2 0 8 7           3
    8 6 3 8 7 5 8 9 4 7       0
    2   2       5             9
  1 4   4     4 1             2
1 0 2     3 3 0 4 3 4 5 5 8 3 1
8 0 0 4 9 4     1 1             8
9 4 8   7   1 1     4         5
9 4 3   0 4   4       4       9
1 0 6 4 1   1 8 7       3     4
4 0 1   9     8   2       4   3
7 2 8   8 8   4 4   9       7
4 7 7   2   0 2   3   0
2 8 3   4     2     4   3
0 9 9 3 0 7 7 0 2 0 1 9
  0   5 0 4 4 9 9 4 1 8 1 1 4
```

Number Search Solutions

FIND THE NUMBERS
Puzzle # 5

	5	4	3	3	4	0	7	4						9
		7			8	7	8	8	0	7	2	0	7	
	7	0	9	4	1	5	7	0	4	2				0
5				1			0	7	0	0				1
8		0	1	2	3	0			5	1	6	1		4
1					0	1		1	8	4	4	0	8	
4	8	7	4	1	8	7	9	8	4	4	1	5	5	8
9		9					8			7	1	8	4	0
0			8					5	9		0	4	5	
7	4	2	1	0	7	7	0	3	2	0	7		8	3
			0		2						2		1	
9	8	2	4	3	0	1	4	6	0	7			8	
				3	9	8	2	4	3	4	0	7		
				0	2	8	9	0	0	3	0			
	1	8	0	9	4	8	7	0	9	3	4	8	7	4

FIND THE NUMBERS
Puzzle # 6

8		3	3		4	1	9	3	4	0	6	4	7	5
	3	3	4	8	5	8	9	3	4	3	8			
	8	4		9	8	8	3	8	9	0	1	1	4	3
3	3	4	8	9	0	3	8	9	8	4	3			5
8	9			8		2	4							4
8	4			8		8	2					3	7	
2	6	6			2		9	8				8	8	
0	7		0			4		8	8			7	4	
8	0			9			3		4	2		4	3	
8	9			0	3	4	3	4	2	4	0	8	2	3
8	8			0	8	8	4	2	8	0	9	4		
4	4		2	4	8	1	7	4	9	3	8	8	1	
3	3	1	0	8	9	3	4	3	8	8	4	7	4	
8		1	0	8	0	4	9	1	0	1	1		3	
				5	7	0	2	4	2	4	7	0		

FIND THE NUMBERS
Puzzle # 7

3			3	5									
	4		3	4	0								8
		8	4	8	6								3
		8		8	9	5							9
		0	3	5	9	8	2						4
		3	4	9	2	8	0						7
	9		8	8	8	0	4	3					2
	4		1	9	1	7	5	6					4
	3		2	0	1	9	5						5
5	8	0	3	2	7	4	9	9	4	0		8	4	9
	8			2	2			1	8				
	4			0			4						
		5			1	3							
						4							

FIND THE NUMBERS
Puzzle # 8

7	8												
	8	3			5			4	0	6	4	7	3	
	5	8	3	3	0	4	7	4	0	0	7	8	7	
	1		5	0	8		2					0	9
5	4			9	7	7	6	0				9	4
0	0				0	1	4	3	3			2	5
7	9		9			2	1	3	8	3		7	2
7	5			0			8	1	0	5	8		4	0
2	8				9			1	4	2	2	9	7	9
0	8	5	4	9	9	8	4	8	4	2		0	4	4
7	7		4	1	1	4	1			2	4		5	7
0	8	3	8	8	0	1	3	0	4	2	4	3		1
8	3	0	7	8	4	7	4		7				0
	6												7
													4

Word Search Solutions

Puzzle # 1
ASSORTED WORDS 1

Y	L	B	I	G	E	L	S	H						I
R	M		G	S	F			E	O					N
	O	G		N	L	U	Y	D	G	N				E
	T	B	N		I	E	R	D	E	A	O			F
	O	V	H	I	R	Z	I	N	N	P	L	R		F
	R	I		G	G	E	I	G	I	A	P	I	S	I
S	M	S			I	G	S	S	H	T	R	O	S	C
O	O	E			E	U	A	P	T	U		H	I	
J	U	D				N	H	H	A		R		E	
O	T					C	C	C				E	N	
U	H	S	I	X	P	E	N	C	E	H				T
R	S					Y	L	P	M	A				S
N	C	I	R	C	U	M	C	I	S	E	D			
E					E	N	T	R	A	N	C	I	N	G
D	E	G	N	U	O	R	C	S			T			

Puzzle # 2
ASSORTED WORDS 2

			S	T	S	I	P	R	A	H	R			
G	D	E	I	F	I	R	T	N	E	G		A	P	
	N				E			Y			D	A		
P		I			S	N		E			I	S		
E		D	L			T	L	B			C	T	C	
N		D	E	L	A	H	X	E	A			A	E	R
E			T	A		S		L	R		L	S	O	
T				E	G	W	R	L	L	G	S			U
R					I		A	E		U	E			P
A	G	N	I	L	G	R	U	G	D	I		M	R	I
T	G	N	I	L	L	O	R	Q		D	D			N
I	A	S	B	E	S	T	O	S	S		L	L		G
O			D	E	T	S	U	G	S	I	D	E	O	
N		O	N	I	M	O	L	A	P		D		D	S
S		D	E	I	L	P	P	A	S	I	M			

Puzzle # 3
ASSORTED WORDS 3

	E		S	P	R	O	F	E	S	S	E	S	C	
E		S		R					I	G	L	O	O	
A		S		R	G	E	G				J	N		
R	F		W		E	R	H	N			E		S	
T	L	I		A	C	M	A	S	I			T		I
H	O		C		R	R	M	M	A	U		T		D
L	G	B		I	G	C	E	I	M	W	R	I		E
I	G	A	U	T	O	N	O	M	Y	A	H	E		R
E	E	C			N	I	N	A		R	S			E
S	D	K			D	A	T	V	T		I	I		D
T		D		D	U	D	E	D	I	E	O		A	D
L	E	A	D	S				K	O	N	R	R		N
	T					N		G	S	I				
	E		O	V	A	R	Y			I		I	E	A
	P	T	O	M	A	I	N	E	S	F				S

Puzzle # 4
ASSORTED WORDS 4

	P	R	E	E	X	I	S	T	E	D				
C	C	E	X	T	I	N	G	U	I	S	H	E	R	S
	H	T	I	T	L	I	N	G	X					
	E	A				H	T	S	E	R	A	R		
M	E	A	N	I	N	G	L	E	S	S	L			E
P	R	E	C	T	O	R	S		A			P		X
R	F			D	I	S	R	U	P	T	I	N	G	P
I	U	M	I	N	I	C	A	M	S		H			E
C	L		S	E	Z	I	L	A	R	O	M	E	D	C
E	L	S	W	O	R	G	R	E	V	O			N	T
L	E	Y	L	E	V	I	S	N	E	T	X	E		A
E	S	F	I	B	E	R	B	O	A	R	D			N
S	T			P	E	R	D	I	T	I	O	N	T	
S	S	R	E	K	A	E	R	B	W	A	J			L
Y	A	H	O	O	D	E	L	B	B	U	B			Y

Word Search Solutions

Puzzle # 5
ASSORTED WORDS 5

R	S		Y		T		A	V	A	T	A	R	
A	M		E		Y	L	D	R	A	W	T	U	O
D	A			S	S		D		O				M
I	I				S	T	S	I	T	U	A	L	F	A
A	N				U	R		P		P		S	V
T	S					B	O		M		E	A	E
E	T	B	O	U	L	D	E	R	L		I		L	R
S	R	M		O	I	L	F	I	E	L	D	L	L	I
D	E	C	A	P	S	K	C	A	B	D	E		I	C
	A	L		L		A				N	R	E	K
	M		B		I		T				U	D	S
	S			O		G	W	O	O	L	Y		L
		S	H	I	N	I	N	G	I				B
O	R	A	C	L	I	N	G	S
S	E	Z	T	A	S	R	E	N	A	S	C	E	N	T

Puzzle # 6
ASSORTED WORDS 6

R	E	P	U	B	L	I	C	M	A	Y	D	A	Y	S
S	L	W	O	R	G	K			V	A	G	I	N	A
I	N	T	E	N	D	E	D	S	K	C	I	R	T
	C	O	G			E	R	S	T	R	I	D	E
I	O	E	I	E		P		E	E
N	N	M	G	T	O	S			B	G
C	T	P	O	D	A	L	A	R	M	I	N	G	L	Y
U	R	A		U	E	C	O	R	E		N	A		R
L	A	P			N	L	S	G	E	D		D	R	I
P	V	P				T	S	I	I	T	L		S	P
A	E	E				A		F	C	O	O		P
T	N	D					I		N	A	O	B	E
I	E	O	U	T	R	A	G	I	N	G	O	L	C	R
N	O	I	T	P	E	C	R	E	P	S		C		S
G			L	I	V	E	R	I	E	S

Puzzle # 7
ASSORTED WORDS 7

	F	O	P	O	P	U	L	A	T	I	N	G
I	M	A	N	I	A	R	E	D	R	A	W	I	N	G
	N	R	S	R	R	E	S	E	M	B	L	E	S
P	S	G	A	T	O					E	S	P
R	E	C	R	D	I	P				V	E	U
O	R	Y		A	I	D				I	R	D
B	I	C			I	O	I		B	A	P	D
L	A	L			N	I	O		L	T	E	I
E	L	A			E	N	U	A	H	N	N	P
M	M				D	G	S	A	T	G	E
A	D	E	D	N	U	O	T	S	A	T	N	S	A
T		N			S	S	E	N	E	S	O	L	C
I	G	N	I	T	S	I	X	E	E	R	P		H
C	S	N	O	T	S	E	C	N	E	S	B	A
B	I	N	O	M	I	A	L	T	E	A	S	E	R	S

Puzzle # 8
ASSORTED WORDS 8

	G	N	I	T	S	A	L	R	E	V	E	F
G	N	I	T	A	U	T	N	E	V	E		S	L
D	I	S	S	E	M	I	N	A	T	E	D		H	A
	S	C	O	L	D	I	N	G	O			O	G
E				B			V		D	W	O
L		F			A		E		A	M	N
A	S	E	I	T	L	A	S	L		R		M	E	S
B	I	R	I	U	Q	I	A	D	L	L		A	N
O				R	E	D	N	A	T	S	Y	B
R				B	D	A	Y	C	K
A		M	E	D	D	L	E	R	S	P
T	N	E	M	U	N	O	M		O		T
I	H	E	A	R	T	I	E	S	T	K		I
O	A	C	C	O	M	P	L	I	S	H	E	S	N
N	D	O	C	U	M	E	N	T	I	N	G	R		G

Word Search Solutions

Puzzle # 9
ASSORTED WORDS 9

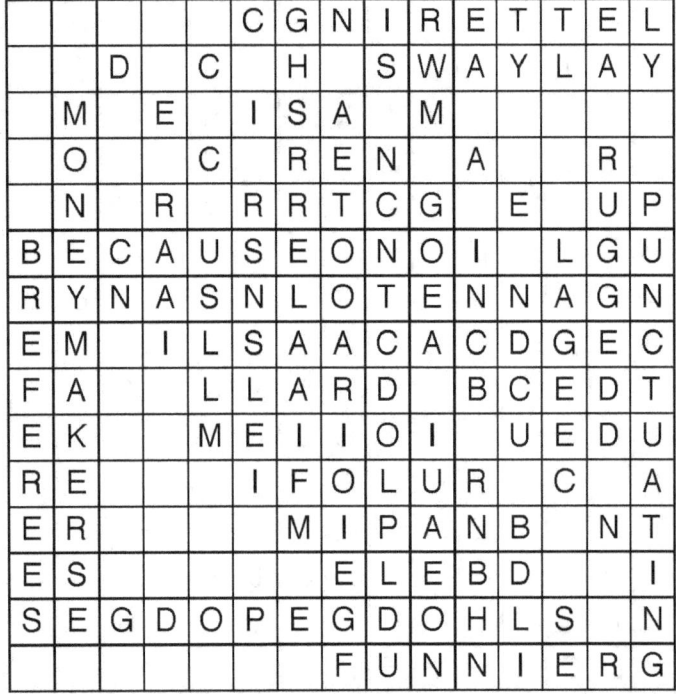

	N	C	O	R	R	E	L	A	T	E	D			T	
T	S	O	G		S	C	I	T	C	E	L	C	E	A	
	R	T	I	N	P	I	C	N	U					N	
C	Y	A	A	T	I	I	S	A	F	B				K	
O	S	T	E	R	A	L	C	Y	P	E	I			F	
N	F	G	I	H	K	L	B	K	L	I	R	L		U	
F		A	N	S	G	S	U	R	A	A	T	N	A	L	
E	B		N	I	O	N	U	S	A	X	T	O	A	H	
D		E		T	T	M	I	M	P	G	I	A	L	L	
E			E		A	A	I	R		A		N	C	S	
R	S			T		S	L	N	E		C		G		
A		C			L		I	E	A	E		N			
T			A			I		Z	R		P		E		
E				P			N	D	E	T	N	I	A	F	
D			Y	D	E	E	R	G	V	I	S	I	N	G	

Puzzle # 10
ASSORTED WORDS 10

		C	O	N	D	U	C	T	I	V	I	T	Y		
P			D	E	N	E	S	S	E	L					
R		G		N	A	M	S	N	I	K					
A		G	N	I	R	E	E	N	A	C	C	U	B	P	
I			D	I	S	T	I	L	L	E	D			A	
S				C	D			B					S	L	
I	D		S	R	A	N	I	M	E	S			U	P	
N	N	E	R	O	T	S	E	C	N	A			N	A	
G	S	C	T	S			K			D			B	T	
	T		U	S		H	Y		O			I	O	E	
	O			B	E		S	K	C	O	R	C	N	D	
	U			O	A	R		A	N			B	N	G	
	T			W		T	O		L	U			E		
	E			S			E	F		S	J		T		
	R		H	U	N	C	H	E	D				S		

Puzzle # 11
ASSORTED WORDS 11

				C	G	N	I	R	E	T	T	E	L
		D		C		H		S	W	A	Y	L	A	Y
	M		E		I	S	A		M					
	O			C		R	E	N		A			R	
	N		R		R	R	T	C	G		E		U	P
B	E	C	A	U	S	E	O	N	O	I		L	G	U
R	Y	N	A	S	N	L	O	T	E	N	N	A	G	N
E	M		I	L	S	A	A	C	A	C	D	G	E	C
F	A			L	L	A	R	D		B	C	E	D	T
E	K		M	E	I	I	O	I		U	E	D	U
R	E			I	F	O	L	U	R		C		A
E	R			M	I	P	A	N	B		N	T
E	S				E	L	E	B	D			I
S	E	G	D	O	P	E	G	D	O	H	L	S	N
					F	U	N	N	I	E	R	G

Puzzle # 12
ASSORTED WORDS 12

	D	I	S	Q	U	A	L	I	F	Y	I	N	G	
W	A	Y	W	A	R	D	L	Y	B					
	N			M	A	T	U	R	I	T	I	E	S	D
	A		R	R	E	T	I	V	N	I			W	I
O	I		E	A		C	A	N	C	E	R	A	S	
R	A	N			T	E			A			S	P	
I	D		T	G	C	L	D		C			H	A	
G	S	E	T	E	N	O	U	N	L			T	R	
I	T		E	N	R	I	D	A	E		W	E	A	
N		U		P	I	C	Y	E	S	O	O	H	C	T
A			R		E	A	O	O	X	S		E	H	E
T			B		S	U	M	V		A	W	S	S	
I				O		T	Q	S	N		E			
N	E	T	A	I	R	T	A	P	X	E	O	D		
G	O	V	E	R	N	E	S	S	E	S		C		

Word Search Solutions

Puzzle # 13
ASSORTED WORDS 13

```
P . . C . . S E C A L P S I M
R . . R . . . Y P A C K E R W
E X C A V A T I O N S . . . E
A R R F . . S E L B M U T S E
C E E T T . F N D E N O H I .
H U W S R S S L S E . M . . N
E N A M O W R E D L A . O . G
R I R A P . . E I T A T . H R
S O D N I . . I E Z E U L . E
. N S S S . N . N O E S Y O .
. S . H M . G . . A O L A C .
. . D I S A S T E R . C B S C
. . . P . N E M S S E H C . U
. P A N T A L O O N S . . U R
I N S T R U M E N T I N G . B
```

Puzzle # 14
ASSORTED WORDS 14

```
S E I F I S L A F . . . . . .
. B P T A N N E S T . . . . .
. U . L H C T A P S I D . . .
S T . N E S T E P M U R T S .
R T . S O C P . . . M . M . .
P O A . N R T U S A N D I E R
R C T E R O T R R J A P I N G
O K . C L O O H U I . . D G .
J S . . E C T L E M O . . A U
E . E . . T . A A R . U . C T
C . D . . E . D S N . S I T .
T . . U . . D . E . E . O E .
O . . . L . . . . R . R U R .
R S O M N O L E N C E P . S S
S . G O U R M A N D S . . . .
```

Puzzle # 15
ASSORTED WORDS 15

```
. A Y E P . . . G . . P . .
. T S . T Z A M P U L S . E
. D S E S I I E . . U . R P
. . E E N T R R H . T . S A
. . R Z L I A A E C E . E U
. . T . I B G O L P N . V P
. . . E H . I B U U . E E .
C I T P Y R C . R R N A . R R
. . . . O E . O O A P E I .
D E R E B O S W T . B T R D Z
S C O R N F U L S A . A O G E
. I M P A C T . R C . . M S
. D E P I N S I S O N P Y H
. P A N D E R I N G F . . .
I N A P P R O P R I A T E .
```

Puzzle # 16
ASSORTED WORDS 16

```
C I R O M O H P O S T . . . .
. S . . L I N K A G E S . . .
S T N A T L U S N O C N . . .
. . O H I G H B A L L T . . .
Y C A L C I T E . S . . . . S
Y R . R G S T . S . Y . . . A
E O R E N R A Y P S E U L . C
T L T E S I E I F M . B . . I
R . L P I E L G C I A . O . D
. I . A M K R D A O V T . . I
. U . V E O V D R S I S . . F
. Q . . R M E E O S V Y . . .
P I G G I S H N E S S M F A I
. S E T A I D U P E R . . . N
R A C Q U E T B A L L S G . .
```

Word Search Solutions

Puzzle # 17
ASSORTED WORDS 17

```
  S R E E D L L I K
  L       E P O C H S
    E   B   Y N O H P
  T S L A R R O C I     C
  T S E   G L A X I A L O
E   S E T   U L S     T R
  X   E N U S E A H     R
G   U   I E C T S B E   E U
T L F D   N E E A   E S C   C
  E I   E   N R X E   R T
    L B   S   U G E R   I
  M U B   K   F     T O F
  I   A E   C O W H A N D S
  E     P S   U     A E
  R     E T   D     L
```

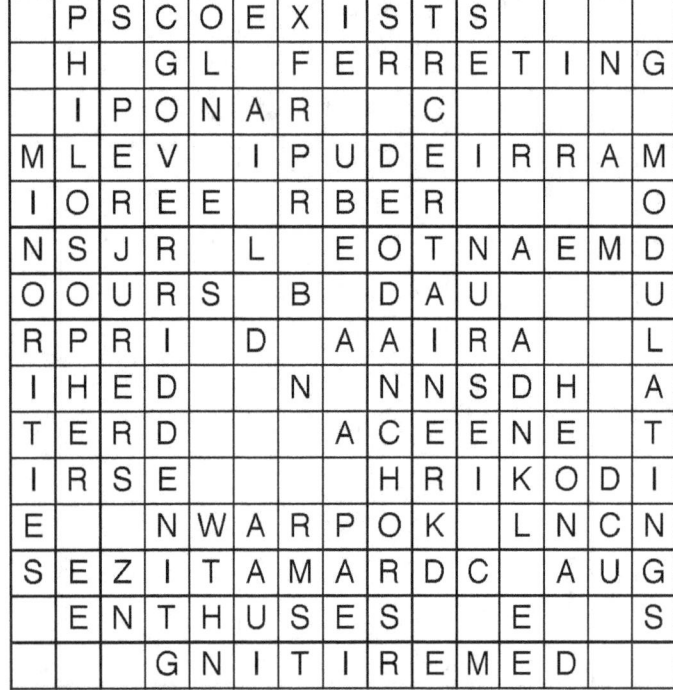

Puzzle # 18
ASSORTED WORDS 18

```
    Y T D E K C I S     C
  Y   R R S E D S P A R T O S
    P B E O I T E P     N U
S   B A R G T G I T U     D N
O E   U R A G A O M A S   O L
M   I S F E I A M L I L S N E
B R   T R F H N B A O L S E S
R   E   I E E T I T L I   D S
E     G   S T R O N E C D
R       N   R A S M G P X A
O     C O A T E R   E   R E R
          M   V C   H   A
  P H O N I E R   D     C   C
T H G I E W R E H T A E F
S N O I T C U R T S N I
```

Puzzle # 19
ASSORTED WORDS 19

```
  P S C O E X I S T S
  H   G L   F E R R E T I N G
  I P O N A R     C
M L E V   I P U D E I R R A M
I O R E E   R B E R         O
N S J R   L   E O T N A E M D
O O U R S   B   D A U       U
R P R I   D   A A I R A     L
I H E D     N   N N S D H   A
T E R D     A C E E N E     T
I R S E       H R I K O D I
E     N W A R P O K   L N C N
S E Z I T A M A R D C   A U G
  E N T H U S E S     E     S
    G N I T I R E M E D
```

Puzzle # 20
ASSORTED WORDS 20

```
      L     E N I R E C Y L G
        I C H A N G E O V E R R
    C D   R   S     L W O R P
R N O   O   A   Y W A I S T H
S E I L B M E S S A         Y
  I D   O   A A S O R E S   P
  G V R H N F I L   R F     E
  H   A O T I L N U E   F   R
  I   E L B D Z U S B     A B
  N     X E   I E T A I   M O
  G       H N   W   T   F E L
G E R M I N A T E D I E   S I
      E B U L L I E N T R H C
D E T C U D N I E N G A   E
C H E C K B O O K D E   B S D
```

Sudoku Solutions

Puzzle # 1

6	1	4	8	9	5	7	2	3
8	9	7	2	3	1	5	4	6
2	5	3	4	6	7	8	9	1
1	8	2	7	5	3	4	6	9
7	3	9	6	4	2	1	8	5
4	6	5	1	8	9	3	7	2
5	4	6	3	2	8	9	1	7
3	7	8	9	1	6	2	5	4
9	2	1	5	7	4	6	3	8

Puzzle # 2

9	5	2	4	1	7	3	6	8
1	7	8	3	9	6	5	4	2
6	4	3	5	8	2	9	7	1
4	9	6	8	2	3	7	1	5
3	8	5	1	7	9	4	2	6
2	1	7	6	5	4	8	9	3
5	3	4	7	6	1	2	8	9
8	6	9	2	4	5	1	3	7
7	2	1	9	3	8	6	5	4

Puzzle # 3

3	5	1	4	7	2	8	9	6
4	6	2	3	9	8	1	5	7
7	9	8	5	6	1	3	4	2
8	3	9	2	4	6	5	7	1
6	1	7	8	5	3	4	2	9
5	2	4	9	1	7	6	3	8
9	8	5	6	2	4	7	1	3
2	7	3	1	8	5	9	6	4
1	4	6	7	3	9	2	8	5

Puzzle # 4

5	6	3	2	9	7	4	8	1
2	1	8	6	5	4	7	3	9
9	7	4	8	3	1	5	6	2
6	4	9	3	7	8	1	2	5
8	2	7	1	4	5	3	9	6
1	3	5	9	6	2	8	7	4
4	8	6	5	2	3	9	1	7
3	5	2	7	1	9	6	4	8
7	9	1	4	8	6	2	5	3

Sudoku Solutions

Puzzle # 5

7	4	2	5	3	8	1	6	9
5	3	6	1	9	2	7	4	8
1	8	9	4	6	7	5	2	3
6	2	4	7	8	3	9	1	5
3	1	7	9	5	4	2	8	6
9	5	8	6	2	1	3	7	4
8	7	1	3	4	9	6	5	2
4	6	3	2	7	5	8	9	1
2	9	5	8	1	6	4	3	7

Puzzle # 6

2	5	1	3	4	9	8	6	7
9	3	6	1	8	7	5	2	4
7	4	8	6	5	2	9	3	1
4	7	3	8	1	6	2	9	5
1	8	2	4	9	5	6	7	3
6	9	5	7	2	3	1	4	8
5	2	7	9	3	8	4	1	6
3	1	9	5	6	4	7	8	2
8	6	4	2	7	1	3	5	9

Puzzle # 7

8	1	2	6	5	7	9	4	3
9	4	5	3	8	1	7	2	6
3	7	6	2	9	4	5	1	8
4	5	9	8	2	6	3	7	1
2	3	1	5	7	9	8	6	4
7	6	8	4	1	3	2	5	9
1	8	7	9	4	2	6	3	5
5	2	3	1	6	8	4	9	7
6	9	4	7	3	5	1	8	2

Puzzle # 8

3	2	1	9	6	4	7	5	8
7	8	4	3	5	1	9	2	6
9	5	6	2	7	8	3	1	4
8	4	3	5	1	6	2	9	7
1	9	7	8	4	2	5	6	3
2	6	5	7	3	9	8	4	1
5	1	8	4	2	3	6	7	9
6	3	2	1	9	7	4	8	5
4	7	9	6	8	5	1	3	2

Sudoku Solutions

Puzzle # 9

2	6	3	5	8	1	7	9	4
1	8	7	4	6	9	5	2	3
4	9	5	3	2	7	6	1	8
9	3	1	8	7	4	2	5	6
8	5	4	6	9	2	3	7	1
6	7	2	1	3	5	8	4	9
7	2	6	9	4	8	1	3	5
3	1	9	7	5	6	4	8	2
5	4	8	2	1	3	9	6	7

Puzzle # 10

2	4	7	9	5	3	1	6	8
1	6	5	8	4	2	9	3	7
8	9	3	7	6	1	5	2	4
5	2	4	3	9	8	6	7	1
9	3	1	4	7	6	2	8	5
6	7	8	2	1	5	4	9	3
7	5	2	6	8	4	3	1	9
4	8	6	1	3	9	7	5	2
3	1	9	5	2	7	8	4	6

Puzzle # 11

8	2	9	7	6	3	1	5	4
7	6	3	1	4	5	9	2	8
5	4	1	8	9	2	6	3	7
6	9	8	3	2	1	4	7	5
2	5	4	9	7	6	3	8	1
3	1	7	5	8	4	2	9	6
1	7	5	4	3	9	8	6	2
9	8	6	2	1	7	5	4	3
4	3	2	6	5	8	7	1	9

Puzzle # 12

5	4	3	1	9	7	8	6	2
1	7	2	4	6	8	3	5	9
8	6	9	2	3	5	7	1	4
6	8	4	7	1	9	2	3	5
2	9	5	3	8	6	4	7	1
3	1	7	5	2	4	9	8	6
4	3	8	6	5	2	1	9	7
7	5	1	9	4	3	6	2	8
9	2	6	8	7	1	5	4	3

Sudoku Solutions

Puzzle # 13

6	8	2	1	3	5	7	4	9
7	4	5	2	8	9	3	1	6
1	9	3	4	7	6	5	8	2
9	6	4	3	5	8	2	7	1
2	3	8	7	1	4	6	9	5
5	1	7	9	6	2	4	3	8
8	2	9	5	4	7	1	6	3
4	5	1	6	9	3	8	2	7
3	7	6	8	2	1	9	5	4

Puzzle # 14

9	1	5	6	3	2	8	7	4
4	2	8	7	5	1	9	6	3
7	3	6	4	8	9	5	2	1
8	5	1	9	4	6	2	3	7
6	9	4	3	2	7	1	8	5
2	7	3	5	1	8	6	4	9
5	8	7	1	6	3	4	9	2
1	6	9	2	7	4	3	5	8
3	4	2	8	9	5	7	1	6

Puzzle # 15

7	2	5	4	6	8	1	3	9
1	8	6	5	9	3	2	7	4
9	4	3	1	7	2	5	8	6
4	1	2	7	3	6	9	5	8
3	9	7	8	1	5	4	6	2
6	5	8	9	2	4	3	1	7
5	7	4	3	8	9	6	2	1
2	3	1	6	4	7	8	9	5
8	6	9	2	5	1	7	4	3

Puzzle # 16

6	3	9	2	1	5	8	4	7
1	7	8	6	4	3	5	9	2
5	2	4	8	7	9	6	1	3
2	8	5	3	9	1	7	6	4
4	1	7	5	6	2	9	3	8
3	9	6	4	8	7	2	5	1
8	5	2	9	3	4	1	7	6
7	6	3	1	5	8	4	2	9
9	4	1	7	2	6	3	8	5

Sudoku Solutions

Puzzle # 17

4	6	1	9	3	5	8	2	7
9	7	2	8	1	4	6	3	5
8	3	5	7	6	2	4	1	9
7	2	8	6	4	1	9	5	3
6	5	4	3	2	9	7	8	1
1	9	3	5	7	8	2	6	4
5	1	6	4	8	7	3	9	2
2	8	7	1	9	3	5	4	6
3	4	9	2	5	6	1	7	8

Puzzle # 18

3	4	1	9	8	7	6	2	5
7	6	8	5	2	1	4	3	9
2	9	5	3	6	4	8	7	1
5	8	3	7	9	6	1	4	2
6	1	2	4	3	8	5	9	7
9	7	4	2	1	5	3	8	6
1	3	7	6	4	2	9	5	8
4	2	6	8	5	9	7	1	3
8	5	9	1	7	3	2	6	4

Puzzle # 19

1	9	7	4	3	6	5	2	8
3	8	4	2	5	7	6	1	9
2	5	6	9	8	1	4	3	7
9	3	2	5	6	4	7	8	1
5	4	1	7	9	8	3	6	2
7	6	8	1	2	3	9	5	4
8	7	5	3	4	2	1	9	6
4	2	3	6	1	9	8	7	5
6	1	9	8	7	5	2	4	3

Puzzle # 20

4	9	7	5	1	8	3	2	6
1	2	3	7	4	6	9	5	8
5	6	8	3	9	2	7	4	1
2	3	9	8	6	5	4	1	7
6	1	5	4	7	9	8	3	2
7	8	4	2	3	1	6	9	5
3	5	1	6	8	4	2	7	9
9	7	6	1	2	3	5	8	4
8	4	2	9	5	7	1	6	3

Thank you so much for your
purchase! I hope you enjoy your
activity book.
Please check out our other
puzzle books available on Amazon.

Warm regards,

Little Doggy Press